Fast Facts for the NEW NURSE PRACTITIO[...] *What You Really Need to Know in a Nutshell*, Aktan

Fast Facts for the ER NURSE: *Emergency Room Orientation in a Nutshell, 2e,* Buettner

Fast Facts for the ANTEPARTUM AND POSTPARTUM NURSE: *A Nursing Orientation and Care Guide in a Nutshell,* Davidson

Fast Facts About PRESSURE ULCER CARE FOR NURSES: *How to Prevent, Detect, and Resolve Them in a Nutshell*, Dziedzic

Fast Facts for the GERONTOLOGY NURSE: *A Nursing Care Guide in a Nutshell*, Eliopoulos

Fast Facts for the CLINICAL NURSE MANAGER: *Managing a Changing Workplace in a Nutshell*, Fry

Fast Facts for EVIDENCE-BASED PRACTICE: *Implementing EBP in a Nutshell*, Godshall

Fast Facts About NURSING AND THE LAW: *Law for Nurses in a Nutshell,* Grant, Ballard

Fast Facts for the L&D NURSE: *Labor & Delivery Orientation in a Nutshell,* Groll

Fast Facts for the FAITH COMMUNITY NURSE: *Implementing FCN/Parish Nursing in a Nutshell*, Hickman

Fast Facts for the CARDIAC SURGERY NURSE: *Everything You Need to Know in a Nutshell*, Hodge

Fast Facts for the CLINICAL NURSING INSTRUCTOR: *Clinical Teaching in a Nutshell, 2e,* Kan, Stabler-Haas

Fast Facts for the WOUND CARE NURSE: *Practical Wound Management in a Nutshell*, Kifer

Fast Facts About EKGs FOR NURSES: *The Rules of Identifying EKGs in a Nutshell,* Landrum

Fast Facts for the CRITICAL CARE NURSE: *Critical Care Nursing in a Nutshell*, Landrum

Fast Facts for the TRAVEL NURSE: *Travel Nursing in a Nutshell*, Landrum

Fast Facts for the SCHOOL NURSE: *School Nursing in a Nutshell*, Loschiavo

Fast Facts About CURRICULUM DEVELOPMENT IN NURSING: *How to Develop & Evaluate Educational Programs in a Nutshell,* McCoy, Anema

Fast Facts for DEMENTIA CARE: *What Nurses Need to Know in a Nutshell*, Miller

Fast Facts for HEALTH PROMOTION IN NURSING: *Promoting Wellness in a Nutshell*, Miller

Fast Facts for the MEDICAL OFFICE NURSE: *What You Really Need to Know in a Nutshell*, Richmeier

Fast Facts About the GYNECOLOGICAL EXAM FOR NURSE PRACTITIONERS: *Conducting the GYN Exam in a Nutshell,* Secor, Fantasia

Fast Facts for the STUDENT NURSE: *Nursing Student Success in a Nutshell,* Stabler-Haas

Fast Facts for CAREER SUCCESS IN NURSING: *Making the Most of Mentoring in a Nutshell*, Vance

Fast Facts for DEVELOPING A NURSING ACADEMIC PORTFOLIO: *What You Really Need to Know in a Nutshell*, Wittmann-Price

Fast Facts for the CLASSROOM NURSING INSTRUCTOR: *Classroom Teaching in a Nutshell*, Yoder-Wise, Kowalski

Forthcoming FAST FACTS Books

Fast Facts for the MEDICAL–SURGICAL NURSE: *Clinical Orientation in a Nutshell,* Ciocco

Fast Facts for the NEONATAL NURSE: *A Nursing Orientation and Care Guide in a Nutshell,* Davidson

Fast Facts for the LONG-TERM CARE NURSE: *A Guide for Nurses in Nursing Homes and Assisted Living Settings,* Eliopoulos

Fast Facts for the RADIOLOGY NURSE: *An Orientation and Nursing Care Guide in a Nutshell,* Grossman

Fast Facts for the ADOLESCENT HEALTH NURSE: *Nursing Care in a Nutshell,* Herrman

Fast Facts for the ONCOLOGY NURSE: *Oncology Nursing Orientation in a Nutshell,* Lucas

Fast Facts for STROKE CARE NURSING: *An Expert Care Guide in a Nutshell,* Morrison

Fast Facts for the PEDIATRIC NURSE: *An Orientation Guide in a Nutshell,* Rupert, Young

FAST FACTS FOR THE ANTEPARTUM AND POSTPARTUM NURSE

Michele R. Davidson, PhD, CNM, CFN, RN, CPS, holds a doctorate in nursing administration and health care policy from George Mason University, where she is currently an associate professor of nursing and serves as the coordinator of the nursing PhD program. Dr. Davidson completed a Master's of Science in Nursing from Case Western Reserve University, obtained her certification as a certified nurse midwife, and has a special interest in high-risk obstetrics and women's mental health issues, including postpartum depression and psychosis.

Dr. Davidson has published over 50 papers, contributed more than 19 chapters to other authors' textbooks, and published an additional 21 textbooks that she has co-written, including the international bestseller *Old's Maternal-Newborn Nursing and Women's Health Care Across the Lifespan* (9th edition), which is translated into nine languages and used throughout the world. Dr. Davidson recently published *A Nurse's Guide to Women's Mental Health Care*, which earned an *American Journal of Nursing* Book Award in 2012 in the category of psychiatric mental-health nursing.

In 2002, Dr. Davidson established the Smith Island Foundation to provide rural health care education and screening programs and children's programming to a small island community in the Chesapeake Bay area. She subsequently developed an immersion clinical practicum for students to participate in rural community health on Smith Island. She is also the author of the children's book *Stowaways to Smith Island*.

FAST FACTS FOR THE ANTEPARTUM AND POSTPARTUM NURSE

A Nursing Orientation and Care Guide in a Nutshell

Michele R. Davidson, PhD, CNM, CFN, RN, CPS

Springer Publishing Company, LLC
11 West 42nd Street
New York, NY 10036
www.springerpub.com

Acquisitions Editor: Elizabeth Nieginski
Composition: S4Carlisle Publishing Services

ISBN: 978-0-8261-6886-3
e-book ISBN: 978-0-8261-6887-0

13 14 15 16 / 5 4 3 2 1

The author and the publisher of this Work have made every effort to use sources believed to be reliable to provide information that is accurate and compatible with the standards generally accepted at the time of publication. Because medical science is continually advancing, our knowledge base continues to expand. Therefore, as new information becomes available, changes in procedures become necessary. We recommend that the reader always consult current research and specific institutional policies before performing any clinical procedure. The author and publisher shall not be liable for any special, consequential, or exemplary damages resulting, in whole or in part, from the readers' use of, or reliance on, the information contained in this book. The publisher has no responsibility for the persistence or accuracy of URLs for external or third-party Internet websites referred to in this publication and does not guarantee that any content on such websites is, or will remain, accurate or appropriate.

Library of Congress Cataloging-in-Publication Data

Davidson, Michele R., author.
Fast facts for the antepartum and postpartum nurse : a nursing orientation and care guide in a nutshell / Michele R. Davidson.
p. ; cm. — (Fast facts)
Includes bibliographical references and index.
ISBN 978-0-8261-6886-3 — ISBN 0-8261-6886-8 — ISBN 978-0-8261-6887-0 (e-book)
I. Title. II. Series: Fast facts (Springer Publishing Company)
[DNLM: 1. Obstetrical Nursing—methods. 2. Neonatal Nursing—methods. 3. Perinatal Care—methods. 4. Pregnancy Complications—nursing. WY 157]
RG951
618.2'0231--dc23
2013040617

Printed in the United States of America by Gasch Printing.

For my mother,
Geraldine Gross Lewis,
who is the most amazing friend, supporter, confidant, mentor, and guide, and who has been an incredible mother who unselfishly and wholeheartedly has given more than any daughter could expect, hope for, or dream of. Our journey in this life together has been filled with highs and lows, and joys and tears, and through it all, you have persisted with unconditional love, grace, kindness, and humility.

Contents

Preface

This book provides a basic reference for nurses caring for women and their families during the antepartum and postpartum periods. During pregnancy and in the initial first 6 weeks following birth, women undergo dramatic physiological and psychosocial changes. Families experience dramatic transformations as roles develop and change during these transition periods. Nurses specializing in the care of these families are in a unique position to provide holistic care to ensure optimal health for both the mother and her newborn. In-depth knowledge of the physiological changes that occur during pregnancy and in the postpartum period enables the nurse to detect possible complications that warrant additional assessment. Early identification of risk factors and complications can help prevent adverse maternal and fetal outcomes.

Nurses continue to function as valued members of a collaborative health care team. In this book, the term *clinician* is used because certified nurse midwifes, obstetricians, and perinatologists all work together in the care of women during the antepartum and postpartum periods. Certified nurse midwives often care for low-risk women. In 2009, 8.1% of women in the United States were delivered by a certified nurse midwife or a certified midwife. As health care changes continue to evolve, the number of births attended by nurse midwives will likely increase.

Societal trends have led a number of women to choose to delay having children well into the third or fourth decade of life, choosing to delay childbearing to first establish a career. Some of these women who were once unable to conceive are now aided by assistive technology, which leads to multiple births that are often considered high-risk pregnancies. Due to advanced maternal age, there are often preexisting medical conditions that make a greater number of women at risk for adverse obstetrical outcomes.

Advancements in obstetrical care practices have led to complex care decisions for families during the antepartum period. Nurses must possess excellent communication skills and knowledge of complex procedures and explanations in order to provide in-depth teaching to families. The antepartum and postpartum periods represent the most vulnerable periods of a woman's life. For some women, certain choices made during the antepartum and postpartum periods represent life-and-death decisions. While most women experience uneventful healthy pregnancies, a few will experience profound losses and unexpected postpartum events that create sadness and despair. The nurse can provide tremendous support, encouragement, and understanding and may be the only person the woman can confide in during times of intense loss. The antepartum or postpartum nurse who can rejoice in the happiest birth is not the truest asset, but the nurse that can handhold through the deepest sorrow and the saddest tears is the antepartum or postpartum nurse who is most treasured.

The nurse's role is crucial in caring for women with both low- and high-risk obstetrical care needs. While pregnancy and postpartum are typically times of great joy, for the family experiencing a high-risk pregnancy, anxiety and ambivalence are common. The nurse's role in primary prevention, performing assessments for early detection, frequent screening, ongoing patient education, and individual and family support is crucial. For the woman who has experienced an adverse labor event or postpartum complication, the nurse may be the only source of education and support.

There is no greater joy, responsibility, honor, or blessing than the opportunity to work with growing families during this amazing time in their developing and expanding lives. Each pregnancy, woman, and family is entirely unique, different, and, in some way, utterly amazing. There are those who will pass through a nurse's life uneventfully and, although it is almost sad to say, will likely be, well . . . forgotten, blending in with the many memories that merge together in the days that will eventually create the weeks, months, and years that knit together a nursing career. It is my hope that you encounter many families who permanently imprint themselves on your heart and soul; that vivid images you randomly recall continue to instill in you a passion that inspires you to wake up each day, providing you with the reason to continue to care for families during this crucial time period in their lives!

Michele R. Davidson

Acknowledgments

During my years as a practicing certified nurse midwife, I was blessed to deliver over 1,000 babies and care for thousands more families. Throughout that time, I was acutely aware of the sacred gift I had been given and valued the many tremendous experiences as I awaited the arrival of many precious lives. While I rejoiced with many families during perhaps the happiest moment of their lives, I was also privileged to care for women with unexpected birth outcomes and fetal losses. It was many of those families who in their darkest hours shared the most intimate and raw feelings of human heartache that have shaped my philosophy of nursing, and of life, and ignited my desire to provide compassionate care to all families as they navigated both the joys and heartache that often come with pregnancy, birth, and the postpartum period. It is with immense thanks and gratitude that I would like to acknowledge all of those families for providing me with the opportunity to share their joys and tears.

Elizabeth Nieginski at Springer Publishing Company has been the utmost professional, supportive editor during the planning, writing, and editing of this book. Elizabeth's kind, easygoing approach makes writing a blissful, easy task. She is encouraging and helpful and has been a true supporter of this book since I initially discussed it with her when she first arrived at Springer.

The creation of exceptionally compassionate mothers who instinctively know how to mother, care for, nurture, and support children throughout their life journey continues to fascinate me and has remained a mystery to me to this day. My own mother, Geraldine Gross Lewis, sadly grew up without parents or a mother figure or a family unit, yet has been an exceptional mother who has always instinctively known when to hold tight and when to let go; who loves and gives of herself unselfishly. She has been a role model, a mentor, a confidant, a friend, and a lifeline to me over the years. Soul mate of the heart, she is the one person I can completely depend on, talk to, and confide in, and she continues to inspire me. She is a rare person in that she continues to put her children and grandchildren above all else in her life. One of my greatest joys has come from seeing her love, care for, and support my four children and provide them with a sense of self-confidence, family, love, and never-wavering encouragement.

Special thanks to my husband, Nathan Davidson, who I often equate to being slightly better than winning the lottery! My father, Harry McPhee, and my "little" brother, Chet McPhee, remain avid supporters of all my work; their ongoing encouragement is frequent and always appreciated. Finally, I could not ask for better teachers and guides on my journey of motherhood than my own amazing children: Hayden, Chloe, Caroline, and Grant, who have taught me more in their short lives than any professional education or professor ever could. They have shown me resilience, compassion, and the meaning of true love. You continue to inspire me in so many ways and I remain forever thankful and grateful for the blessings you bring into my life!

I

Introduction to Antepartum and Postpartum Nursing Practice

The care of women and their families during the antepartum and postpartum periods occurs at a time of significant physiological and psychological changes for both. Various policies and procedures are in use to provide safe and competent care to the woman and her family during the childbearing period. Nurses need to utilize evidence-based practice guidelines to provide safe individualized care for these women. Culturally sensitive care is imperative; nurses should be sensitive to the different types of families and familiarize themselves with specific needs of varying families.

Today's nurses are challenged more than ever to care for increasingly high-risk women during the childbearing period. Proper identification of risk factors can play a huge role in providing appropriate care, guiding patient teaching, and implementing interventions that can help reduce modifiable risk factors. These high-risk conditions can create complex ethical implications as nurses provide holistic care to mothers, families, fetuses, and newborns.

After reading this chapter, the nurse will be able to:

1. Identify the key components of policies and procedures that should be universally consistent in order to provide safe and competent care to the woman and her family
2. Discuss the importance of providing evidence-based care
3. Describe the importance of culturally appropriate care
4. Name the different types of families and specific needs that often impact various types of families
5. Identify components of a family assessment
6. Compare and contrast the criteria that identify a woman as low risk or high risk in the antepartum and postpartum periods
7. Differentiate the ethical implications of caring for new families including mothers, fetuses, and newborns

EQUIPMENT

The types of equipment for antepartum and postpartum care vary and will be identified within each chapter of the text.

NURSING CARE AS DIRECTED BY POLICIES AND PROCEDURES

In current nursing practice, antepartum and postpartum care practices are directed by various policies and procedures. Utilizing established policies and procedures ensures that there is a systematic approach to ongoing assessment, interventions, and documentation within the facility. Regardless of the setting, nurses should familiarize themselves with the agency policies and procedures, which should provide the following:

- A purpose for the procedure and identification of when the procedure is appropriate
- Equipment needed
- Clarification of specific responsibilities for each team member
- Specific step-by-step actions written in clear, concise terminology

- A rationale that is evidence-based for each step of the procedure
- References provided within the policy and procedure document
- Dating and identification of the individual who prepared the procedure
- Evidence of committee approval or peer review
- Review and updating of procedures at regular intervals

EVIDENCE-BASED PRACTICE CARE

The use of evidence-based practice care (EBPC) is now universally embraced in nursing and health care as a multidisciplinary approach to providing care based on research findings that support specific care measures. The research should meet a minimum set of standards and rigor so broad applicability can occur. When evaluating materials for the development of EBPC, nurses should utilize appropriate information sources including:

- Research findings that appear in peer-reviewed sources
- Research that has been evaluated and approved by an institutional review board to ensure protection of patient rights
- Studies that utilize appropriate research methods in their design and application
- Inclusion of web-based materials from reliable sources such as government-based resources or professional practice associations with credibility and reliability (e.g., Centers for Disease Control and Prevention, National Institutes of Health, American College of Nurse Midwives, Association of Women's Health, Obstetric and Neonatal Nurses)

As nursing roles continue to evolve, the use of nurse specialists can be an invaluable resource for the ongoing development and evaluation of established policies and procedures. Nurses who specialize in the development of policies and procedures and the incorporation of EBPC include:

- Doctorally prepared nurses (DNPs, PhDs)
- Advanced practice nurses (CNP, CNM, CRNA, CNS)
- Master's-prepared nurse educators
- Research nurses

CULTURAL COMPETENCE AND SENSITIVITY

Cultural competence refers to an understanding of the patient from a holistic perspective and provides care that incorporates the nurse's skills, knowledge, and attitudes in a framework to support the patient's individuality. As diversity increases, the need for cultural competence and culturally sensitive care is essential.

Culturally sensitive care occurs when a nurse has a basic understanding of and possesses a constructive attitude toward the health beliefs and traditions among diverse cultural groups. Cultural competence and culturally sensitive care help to establish trust, provide a platform to identify effective patient teaching strategies, and increase patient satisfaction and compliance. Generalized recommendations to ensure that care is culturally sensitive include:

- Providing services in the patient's native language
- Respecting gender issues such as modesty and whenever possible requests for a specific provider based on gender due to cultural or religious beliefs
- Awareness that specific faith and religious beliefs could impact care and compliance with treatment modalities
- Respect for dietary practices
- Understanding that certain mannerisms and interactions may vary from one culture to another
- Identification of certain family members as key decision makers
- Providing reassurance that individualized beliefs of health and wellness are recognized

FAST FACTS in a NUTSHELL

The United States is one of the most culturally diverse countries in the world in terms of race, ethnicity, religion, culture, and sexual orientation.

Types of Families

In the 1950s, the typical American family was the nuclear family consisting of a father, mother, and their children. In modern society, the nuclear family is no longer the most common type of family unit. While traditional definitions have centered on the inclusion of parents and their children as the basic definition, others have focused solely on family members that are biologically related. The United States Census Bureau has expanded its definition to include two or more individuals living together that are related by birth, marriage, adoption, or who are residing together (United States Census Bureau, 2013). Table 1.1 lists types of historically traditional families, the members of those families, and special needs that various types of families may encounter.

TABLE 1.1 Types of Historically Traditional Families

Type of Family	Members of Family	Special Needs of Family
Nuclear Family	Mother, father, children	Mother *may* feel isolated due to lack of adult interaction while raising family; if previously employed, may miss previous work activities and peer interactions; and may feel pressure to be the "perfect mother." One income may create economic strain, especially if mother was previously employed.
Dual-Career Family	Mother, father, children	Parents may feel stressors with balancing work and child care responsibilities. Family may feel that work takes precedence over family needs. Child-care issues can create anxiety and stress.

TABLE 1.2 Families Without Children

Type of Family	Members of Family	Special Needs of Family
Childless Family	Two partners who do not have children but typically have a desire to have children	Typically a family who has been unable to have children despite desiring children. May or may not have attempted to conceive through assistive technology. Some may have considered adoption. May feel a sense of loss, jealousy, sadness, or despair due to inability to have children.
Childfree Family	Two partners who choose not to have children and typically do not desire children	May feel social pressure because of societal expectations to have children. May encounter circumstances where others voice disagreement with choice not to have children.

While some couples choose to have children, others either may be unable to have children or may wish to remain without children. Table 1.2 presents the types of families that do not include children.

Families that include members beyond the parents and their children are considered extended families. In recent times, extended families have been formed for multiple reasons, including economic reasons. Different types of extended families are included in Table 1.3.

TABLE 1.3 Types of Extended Families

Type of Family	Members of Family	Special Needs of Family
Extended Family	A couple who resides with other family members, which may include parents, siblings, or other family members	May have differences in decision making including division of household chores and economic responsibilities, and child-rearing authority. Common in immigrant families.

(continued)

TABLE 1.3 Types of Extended Families *(continued)*

Type of Family	Members of Family	Special Needs of Family
Extended Kin Network	Two related nuclear families of primary or unmarried kin that live in close proximity to each other	Often share a social support network, goods, and services, which can result in dependence on each other and less interaction with outsiders. May not use community resources due to the ability to rely on kin network.

Single-parent families make up a considerable number of families in the United States, with such families headed by women being much more common than single-parent father-headed families. The different types of single-parent families are included in Table 1.4.

TABLE 1.4 Types of Single-Parent Families

Type of Family	Members of Family	Special Needs of Family
Traditional Single-Parent Family	Typically one parent and a child or children residing together that has resulted from divorce, separation, death of other parent, or abandonment	Most are female-headed families. Often faced with social isolation, lack of emotional support, economic strain, child-care issues, and lack of support or input from others for child-related decisions.
Planned Single-Parent Family	A single parent who desires and facilitates the birth or adoption of child outside of a cohabitating relationship with the intent to parent without a partner. The vast majority are women who achieve pregnancy via planned sexual intercourse with a known partner/donor or donor artificial insemination	Men desiring to become a planned single parent face additional obstacles since adoption or a surrogate pregnancy is needed. May face scrutiny from family members or peers on decision to become planned single parent. Emotional support issues, child care issues, and questions from children regarding absence of other parent may occur.

TABLE 1.5 Types of Postdivorce Families

Type of Family	Members of Family	Special Needs of Family
Stepparent Family	A biological parent and child or children and a new spouse who may or may not have children	Transitions with new parents can cause conflict between children and parents and spouses. Preexisting strained relationship from other biological parent commonly occurs. Financial conflicts on shared expenses between stepparent family and other parent also commonly occur. Visitation with other parent can also result in conflicts.
Binuclear Family	A postdivorced family in which the children are now part of two nuclear households in which they alternate between the two family units, typically in a joint custody arrangement	Legal aspects with shared custody can be complex. Strained relationships between former spouses, lack of effective communication, and inconsistency with expectations between households can create stress and conflicts.

In the 21st century, approximately 46% of all marriages end in divorce. Couples with children who divorce represent different types of postdivorce families (Table 1.5).

Other types of family models are now increasingly more common in American culture. The families included in this group do not fall into the other categories (Table 1.6).

Family Assessment

A family assessment can reveal significant information that can provide insight and help the nurse develop appropriate goals and individualized teaching to the mother and her family. Components of a family assessment should include:

TABLE 1.6 Other Types of Families

Type of Family	Members of Family	Special Needs of Family
Nonmarital Heterosexual Cohabitating Family	An unmarried couple living together who may or may not have children	Lack of legal protections and rights that are afforded to married couples. Elderly couples may choose not to marry due to financial reasons. Couples who do eventually marry after cohabitating have higher divorce rates and report less satisfaction with marital relationship if they do marry (Pew Research Center, 2011).
Gay and Lesbian Families	Either a same-sex couple living together, married, or united under a civil union who may or may not have children or a gay or lesbian single parent living with a child or children	Discrimination still prevalent in some areas, marriages and civil unions often not recognized in other states where legalization does not exist. Legal issues regarding having equal access to partner's legal benefits (insurance coverage, family medical leave, etc.), custody issues, and advocacy in health care decision making for family members are common.

- Names, ages, and sex of all family members within the woman's household
- Type of family as stated by the woman, including roles, family structure, and family values
- Cultural identity as described by the woman that includes customs, traditions, and cultural norms that impact the childbearing period
- Spiritual and faith-based associations including specific religious beliefs, customs, and practices
- Support systems inside and outside of the family including friends, social groups, and community-based resources
- Communication style including identification of language spoken, communication barriers with either verbal or written forms of communication

- Perceptions of health within the family, family health status, presence of disabilities or special needs of family members residing in the household

IDENTIFICATION OF RISK STATUS

Pregnancy is a normal state of wellness and is not considered an illness or alteration in health. Most women remain healthy and active and have uncomplicated pregnancies; however, some women may enter pregnancy with risk factors or may develop high-risk conditions during the antepartum period. It is important to identify women at risk for adverse pregnancy outcomes so appropriate assessments, screenings, and ongoing care management can be utilized to reduce adverse maternal and fetal/newborn outcomes. Women without risk factors who progress and meet the normal developmental milestones of pregnancy are considered low risk.

Risk factors can put the mother and fetus/neonate at risk for adverse outcomes.

- Preexisting risk factors are conditions or factors that existed prior to the pregnancy that may put the mother or fetus/newborn or both at risk for adverse outcomes.
- Pregnancy-related risk factors occur during pregnancy with the onset taking place during the antepartum period that may put the mother, fetus/newborn, or both at risk for an adverse outcome.
- Labor-related risk factors are those that occur in the intrapartum period and create risks for labor and birth and may persist into the postpartum period.
- Postpartum risk factors are those that occur during the postpartum period and can result in adverse clinical outcomes.

ETHICAL ISSUES WHEN CARING FOR MOTHERS AND FETUSES/NEWBORNS

Ethical issues during the childbearing period can result in substantial distress and anxiety for both the family and the health care team. Examples include surrogacy, elective abortion for unplanned pregnancy, multifetal pregnancy reduction, resuscitation of a fetus on the threshold of viability, or the elective termination of a fetus identified as having a genetic defect. Nurses need to understand the basic principles of ethics in order to remain professional, provide appropriate care to the family, and prevent their own values and beliefs from interfering with the care of the woman and her family experiencing a complex ethical issue during pregnancy or in the postpartum period. The following strategies can be used to guide nursing practice:

- Identify your own values and beliefs about the situation
- Support the family in a nonjudgmental manner even if their decision making is in conflict with your own beliefs
- Never attempt to persuade the family based on your own personal beliefs and values
- Provide factual objective information in an unemotional manner
- Provide support to the family utilizing therapeutic communication strategies
- If the family asks the nurse what he or she would do, refrain from offering personal advice
- Elicit support from peers to voice your own feelings and conflicts
- If appropriate, attempt to be reassigned to another patient if a substantial conflict exists between the clinical scenario and your own personal belief system
- Consultation for intervention by social work or psychological support provider may be beneficial
- When appropriate, an ethical consult can be obtained from an ethicist or the ethics committee within the clinical facility

2

Routine Antepartum Assessment

The initial antepartum assessment is a crucial evaluation that provides the health care team with essential information that will dictate the course and treatment approach for the pregnant woman and her family. A thorough physical and psychosocial assessment identifies both actual and potential risk factors that can have a negative impact on the childbearing family. The nurse's role includes obtaining a comprehensive history, performing a physical examination, assisting the practitioner with a detailed pelvic examination, and providing ongoing education and support for the woman and her family.

After reading this chapter, the nurse will be able to:

1. Assess patient and partner history that can impact pregnancy care and outcomes
2. Describe the components of the prenatal history including calculating the due date
3. Discuss basic components of the physical examination and psychosocial assessment

4. Define procedures for obtaining the fetal heart rate
5. List equipment needs for the initial obstetrical examination
6. Name common medications prescribed during routine prenatal care

EQUIPMENT

Reflex hammer, stethoscope, equipment for pelvic exam and Pap smear.

CONSIDERATIONS FOR THE FIRST PRENATAL VISIT INTERVIEW

In a private setting, the nurse obtains a comprehensive medical history that covers each major body system. Most facilities now utilize an electronic medical record with standardized screens and questions; however, it is important to also ask questions that consider cultural norms, language issues, personal values, religious beliefs, educational level, presence of disabilities, and any personal relationships that can impact data collection.

COMPONENTS OF THE MEDICAL HISTORY

The medical history should include a detailed assessment of any health or medical issues the woman or partner has had in the past, along with a detailed review of medication use.

Medication Review

- Current prescription medications
- Over-the-counter medications
- Herbal remedies
- Homeopathic preparations
- Medications taken during the past 3 months
- Prenatal vitamins

Medical Conditions That May Impact Pregnancy

- Diabetes or prediabetes
- Hypertension or prehypertension
- Anemia
- Heart problems or cardiac disease
- Thyroid abnormalities or disorders
- Renal disease
- Diethylstilbestrol (DES) exposure or any previously identified malformations within the reproductive system
- Autoimmune disease
- Sexually transmitted infections, including HIV and hepatitis B or C
- Epilepsy
- Asthma or respiratory disorders
- Bleeding disorders
- Mental health disorders

Prenatal, Labor, and Birth History

- Number of pregnancies
- Pregnancy outcomes (spontaneous abortion, elective termination, preterm birth/term birth, fetal loss)
- Reproductive assistive technologies used to conceive
- Pregnancy course including complications
- Labor and birth history
  - Onset of labor (spontaneous or induced)
  - Medications used in labor
  - History of interventions used in labor (artificial rupture of membranes, augmentation of labor)
  - Mode of birth (vaginal, vacuum, forceps, cesarean delivery, or trial of labor after cesarean)
- Gestational age at birth
- Neonatal factors
  - Weight
  - Apgar scores
  - Complications
  - Birth defects/injuries

- Length of hospitalization
- Neonatal intensive care unit admission and length of stay (if applicable)

- Infant health and complications since birth
- Present health status of child
- Postpartum complications
  - Postpartum hemorrhage
  - Infection
  - Thromboembolic disease
  - Postpartum mental health disorders

Genetic Screening

A personal and family history that includes both the woman's and her partner's data should be obtained. A review of genetic risk factors and known genetic conditions should include:

- Maternal age older than 35 years
- History of spontaneous abortion (and results of any chromosome analysis)
- Chromosomal defects
- History of trisomy (Down syndrome, Turner's syndrome, fragile X syndrome)
- Sickle cell disease/trait
- Tay-Sachs disease
- Cystic fibrosis
- Duchenne muscular dystrophy
- Becker muscular dystrophy
- Huntington's disease
- Thalassemias
- Phenylketonuria
- Inherited thrombophilias

History of Pregnancy Complications

Complications that occur during pregnancy should be documented including the onset of complications, management, and pregnancy outcomes, and should include:

- Iron deficiency anemia
- Polyhydramnios

- Preterm labor/birth
- Premature rupture of membranes
- Gestational diabetes
- Preeclampsia/eclampsia
- Multiple gestation
- Oligohydramnios
- Placental abruption
- Placenta previa

Less common complications should also be assessed including Rh alloimmunization, infections (cytomegalovirus, herpes simplex virus, group B streptococcal infection, human B19 parovirus, *Varicella, Listeria*), subchorionic hemorrhage, cervical insufficiency, habitual abortion, and fetal death.

Labor-Related Complications

- History of labor-related complications
- Abnormal presentation
- Macrosomia
- Nonreassuring fetal status
- Cephalopelvic disproportion
- Adherence of the placenta to the uterine wall (placenta accreta, increta, percreta)
- Anaphylactoid syndrome of pregnancy

BASIC PHYSICAL EXAMINATION

The physical examination for an antepartum examination begins with obtaining a complete set of vital signs, a head-to-toe assessment, and a pelvic exam. A head-to-toe assessment includes a routine physical examination followed by a comprehensive pelvic exam. Pregnancy affects every body system with variations related to hormonal and structural changes that result from increasing uterine size. A head-to-toe physical delineating normal findings, abnormal findings, and pregnancy-related changes is reviewed in Table 2.1. In general, if the nurse notices alterations in vision or hearing, neurological alterations, or changes in a woman's mental status, additional targeted assessments in these areas would be warranted.

TABLE 2.1 Normal Physical Examination Findings With Abnormal and Pregnancy-Related Changes

Body System	Normal Findings	Abnormal Findings	Pregnancy-Related Changes
Skin	Pink, dry, warm to touch, no edema, free from lesions	Pale, bluish hue, mottled, dusky (anemia) Yellow (jaundice) Ulcerations (varicosities, venous insufficiency) Petechiae (hematological disorder) Ecchymosis, bruising with various stages of resolution (physical abuse)	Increase in perspiration Linea nigra Striae Melasma Acne
Oral and Nasal Cavities	Pink mucous membranes	Olfactory loss (cranial nerve damage) Edema of oral cavity (infection) Inflammation (infection) Pallor of mucous membranes (anemia)	Rhinitis of pregnancy (nasal congestion) Epistaxis Hypertrophy of gum tissues Change in sense of smell Pytalism (excessive mucus)
Thyroid	Small, nontender, mobile, without nodules; smooth, palpable on both sides of the trachea with sides being equal in size; auscultation reveals no bruits	Significant enlargement, tenderness, presence of bruits upon palpation (hyperthyroidism)	Slight enlargement can occur with pregnancy

(continued)

TABLE 2.1 Normal Physical Examination Findings With Abnormal and Pregnancy-Related Changes *(continued)*

Body System	Normal Findings	Abnormal Findings	Pregnancy-Related Changes
Lungs	Clear to auscultation in all lung fields with lung sounds present in all lobes, no cough, anterioposterior diameter is smaller than transverse diameter	Chronic cough (emphysema, COPD) Increased AP diameter (lung disease such as emphysema, COPD) Funnel or pigeon chest Wheezing or decreased lung sounds (asthma) Rales, rhonchi, wheezes, pleural rubs (infection, pneumonia) Absence of breath sounds (lung disease, mass, stridor, bronchitis, pulmonary edema), nasal flaring, cyanosis	Shortness of breath, dyspnea on exertion, difficulty breathing with activity (increased uterine size) Increased respiratory rate
Breasts	Enlarged size, darkened nipples and areola, prominent superficial veins, striae	Discrete mass, pain, rash	Increased nodularity Colostrum develops at 12 weeks Breast tenderness

(continued)

TABLE 2.1 Normal Physical Examination Findings With Abnormal and Pregnancy-Related Changes (*continued*)

Body System	Normal Findings	Abnormal Findings	Pregnancy-Related Changes
Heart	Normal rate, rhythm, and normal S1 and S2	Enlargement, trills, irregular beats, gallop or extra sounds (cardiac disease)	Increased heart rate Palpitations Short systolic murmurs (flow murmurs)
Abdomen	Soft, nondistended, no masses Normal bowel sounds Liver nonpalpable Flat abdomen becomes rotund with uterine growth Fetal heart heard via Doppler after 12 gestational weeks with fetal heart rate 110–160 bpm	Firm (constipation) Guarding (anxiety, ticklishness, possible ectopic) Pain (constipation, ectopic pregnancy, appendicitis) Mass (ectopic pregnancy, carcinoma)	Uterus palpable above the symphysis pubis after 12 weeks Halfway between symphysis and umbilicus at 16 weeks At the umbilicus at 20 weeks Three finger breaths above umbilicus at 28 weeks Just below sternum at 36 weeks Fundal measurement equal to or +/– 2 centimeters after 20 weeks when measuring in centimeters from the pubic bone to the top of the fundus Constipation Diastasis

(*continued*)

TABLE 2.1 Normal Physical Examination Findings With Abnormal and Pregnancy-Related Changes *(continued)*

Body System	Normal Findings	Abnormal Findings	Pregnancy-Related Changes
Extremities	Able to move all extremities without discomfort, full ROM, 2+ pulses palpable, negative Homans 'sign, negative or mild edema, 2+ reflexes	Pain in wrists (carpel tunnel syndrome) Pain in legs (varicosities, deep vein thrombosis, severe edema) Positive Homans 'sign (deep vein thrombosis), marked edema (preeclampsia), unpalpable/diminished pulses (arterial deficiency), hyperreflexia or clonus (preeclampsia)	Carpel tunnel syndrome Varicosities Pregnancy-related edema Palmar erythema
Spine/Gait	Concave cervical, concave thoracic, concave lumbar in early pregnancy	Abnormal spine configuration (scoliosis), kyphosis (scoliosis), uneven shoulders or iliac crest (spinal abnormalities)	Lordosis in later pregnancy Wider spaced walk with waddling gait Backache

AP, anterioposterior; COPD, chronic obstructive pulmonary disease; ROM, range of motion.

COMPONENTS OF THE PELVIC EXAM

- Visual inspection of the external genitalia
- Insertion of the speculum
- Vaginal assessment
- Pap smear
- Cultures
- Bimanual examination
- Ovarian assessment
- Pelvimetry (Figure 2.1)

Specific data obtained from a pelvic examination are included in Table 2.2.

FAST FACTS in a NUTSHELL

Certain women may be more uncomfortable with pelvic examinations than others. The nurse should ask the woman if she typically finds pelvic examinations "particularly difficult." Women having their first examination or those with limited experiences with pelvic examinations, adolescents, survivors of sexual abuse or sexual assault, women from certain cultures where modesty is common, and women with certain types of physical factors, such as those with physical disabilities or women who experience chronic pain, require additional support, encouragement, and care during the examination process.

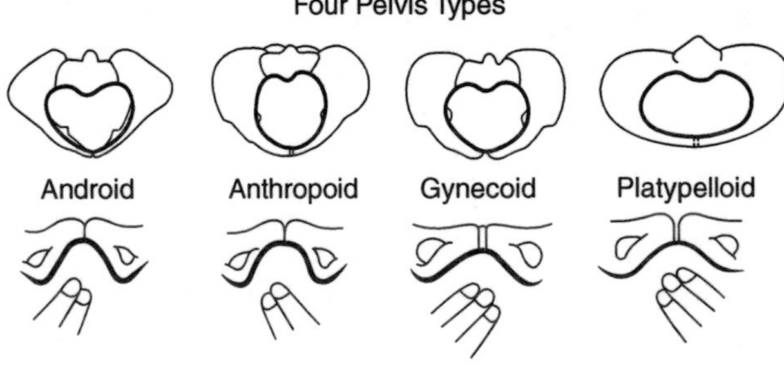

FIGURE 2.1 Different pelvis types.
Source: Four pelvis types. (2011).

TABLE 2.2 Clinical Information Derived From a Comprehensive Pelvic Examination

Anatomical Component	Normal Findings	Abnormal Findings
External Genitalia	Pink in color No lesions Normal female hair distribution Labia majora larger than minor; loose and pigmented Urinary meatus visible Previous episiotomy scar or laceration repair site may be visible	Bruising, pallor Varicosities Hypertrophy of the clitoris Lesions
Vagina	Pink or darkened pink in color White or clear odorless discharge No irritation	Discharge that is foul smelling, yellow, or green Irritation such as burning, itching Visible cystocele
Cervix	Pink in color Smooth Pinpoint opening or slit-like opening in multiparous women Closed No polyps or lesions Soft Positive Chadwick's sign Positive Goodell's sign No bleeding from os	Bleeding from cervical os Cervix that is dilated or effaced Polyps Lesions DES exposure-related abnormalities such as a second infantile cervix Positive chandelier sign (indicates infection)

(*continued*)

TABLE 2.2 Clinical Information Derived From a Comprehensive Pelvic Examination *(continued)*

Anatomical Component	Normal Findings	Abnormal Findings
Uterus	Softened over nonpregnant state Enlargement based on gestational age Nontender, mobile	Fibroids Tenderness
Ovaries	Nontender Presence of small unilateral cyst in first trimester (corpus luteum) No masses	Mass Large cyst Tenderness over ovary and Fallopian tube
Rectum	No lumps No rashes No lesions No excoriations Nontender No hemorrhoids present	Hemorrhoids Fissures Rectal prolapse Mass
Pelvimetry	Gynecoid pelvis Diagonal conjugate > 11.5 cm Obstetric conjugate measured 1.5–2.0 cm from diagonal conjugate Inclination of the sacrum Mobile coccyx Intertuberosity > 8 cm	Android pelvis Anthropoid pelvis Platypelloid pelvis Abnormal pelvic measurements less than desired parameters Abnormal curvature of the sacrum Narrowed pubic arch Fixed coccyx

EQUIPMENT NEEDS FOR A PELVIC EXAMINATION

The nurse assembles all needed equipment prior to the beginning of the examination. Required equipment includes:

- Patient drape or bed sheet
- Patient gown
- Absorbent pad placed beneath the woman's buttocks
- Pap smear collection system (labeled with the woman's name or identification number)
- Pap smear brush, broom, or device to collect cells from the endocervix and ectocervix
- Speculum in various sizes (including a pediatric speculum)
- Wet prep kit (two slides, KOH [potassium hydroxide], saline, slide covers)
- Light source
- Forceps and sterile tenaculum (rarely used)
- Lubricant
- Culture tubes for routine screening (chlamydia, gonorrhea), labeled with name or identification information
- Other culture tubes as needed (mycoplasma, herpes simplex virus), labeled with name or identification information
- Tissues or wipes (for comfort to be provided after the examination)
- Gloves (nonlatex if patient has a latex allergy)
- Trash can with red biohazard bag in place

PSYCHOSOCIAL ASSESSMENT

The psychosocial assessment is as essential as the physical examination findings in obtaining clinically relevant information. It will enable the nurse to build a comprehensive portrait of the woman and her family that supports a holistic family-centered care approach:

- Living environment (type of home and availability of resources within the home)
- Economic status
- Educational history
- Occupation and occupational history, military service
- Health care practices and beliefs
- Use of private or public resources (private insurance, Medicaid, Women, Infants, and Children [WIC], other public assistance programs, social service programs).
- Cultural background and its significance in the lives of the family members
- Religious background and beliefs
- Family values
- History of psychological or mental illnesses including current and past diagnosis and treatment; family history of mental illness
- Smoking status
- Alcohol intake and substance use
- Existence of disabilities and chronic illnesses within the woman or family members
- History of intimate partner violence, sexual assault, abuse
- Support systems and potential future supports after birth
- Adjustment to pregnancy
- Feelings about parenting including experience with infant care and child rearing
- Nutritional history (current diet, dietary restrictions, food allergies, cultural dietary practices)
- Exercise regimen
- Environmental risk factors (chemotherapy, chemicals, radiation)

FAST FACTS in a NUTSHELL

Psychosocial risk factors identified during the initial visit should be used to identify medical and community-based resource needs for the woman and her family.

3

Nursing Care of the Pregnant Woman

Pregnancy is a time of great emotional and physiological adaptation that requires ongoing assessment and monitoring to ensure a healthy outcome for the mother and the fetus. Nursing assessments during pregnancy can identify potential complications that put the mother and fetus at risk. The nurse plays a crucial role in not only ongoing assessment, but in ongoing patient and family education that is vital to ensuring a healthy pregnancy and a satisfying birth experience.

Nursing care of pregnant women is accomplished through regular prenatal care that provides ongoing risk assessment, routine maternal and fetal screening, guidance for health promotion and disease prevention during pregnancy, comfort measures for common discomforts that occur in the gestational period, and guidelines and teaching for the upcoming birth.

After reading this chapter, the nurse will be able to:

1. Identify the frequency and assessment parameters for prenatal visits during pregnancy
2. Discuss how to determine gestational age, uterine growth, and fetal heart tones at each prenatal visit

3. List the recommendations for pregnancy weight gain, nutritional counseling, and exercise
4. Delineate the warning signs that warrant immediate clinician notification
5. Define routine prenatal labs, prenatal screening options, and use of ultrasound in pregnancy
6. Compare and contrast health promotion and risk reduction strategies
7. Define interventions for common discomforts associated with pregnancy
8. Discuss counseling options for labor and birth

EQUIPMENT

Measuring tape, Doppler, urine dipsticks, gestational wheel, scale, blood pressure cuff, thermometer, pulse oximetry.

FREQUENCY OF ANTEPARTUM VISITS

Regular prenatal care is associated with more favorable maternal and infant outcomes. Prenatal care consists of the initial prenatal examination followed by regularly scheduled prenatal visits. Frequency of visits is as follows:

- The initial visit should be scheduled by 8 to 10 gestational weeks
- Follow-up visits are scheduled every 4 weeks until 28 weeks
- During weeks 29 to 36, every 2 weeks
- Weekly visits are scheduled from 37 weeks until delivery

If the woman goes past her expected date of confinement (EDC), more frequent assessments are often required. Women with risk factors may need to be assessed on a more frequent basis.

COMPONENTS OF A ROUTINE ANTEPARTUM VISIT

Determining Gestational Age

A gestational wheel is used to determine the gestational age of the fetus. When using a gestational wheel, the first arrow is placed on the first day of the last menstrual period. The second arrow points to the EDC. The nurse is then able to look at the actual date and determine the gestational age. The gestational age is recorded by the week and additional days; for example 32-4/7 weeks would indicate 32 gestational weeks and 4 days.

Weight Monitoring and Assessment of Edema

Antepartum visits typically begin with obtaining the woman's weight. Recommended weight gain parameters for singleton and multiple gestation pregnancies are based on the woman's body mass index prior to pregnancy and are included in Table 3.1. Women with a rapid weight gain, sudden edema in

TABLE 3.1 Institute of Medicine Recommendations for Weight Gain in Pregnancy

Singleton Pregnancy	Multiple Gestation Pregnancy
• Underweight: Gain 28–40 pounds	• Underweight: No evidence-based guidelines exist
• Normal weight: Gain 25–35 pounds	• Normal weight: Gain 37–54 pounds
• Overweight: Gain 15–25 pounds	• Overweight: Gain 31–50 pounds
• Obese: Gain 11–20 pounds	• Obese: Gain 25–42 pounds

Source: Institute of Medicine (2009).

the face and hands (and to a lesser degree, the lower extremities) should be evaluated for signs of preeclampsia. While edema is common in pregnancy, a sudden onset can be indicative of preeclampsia.

Nutritional Counseling in Pregnancy

Pregnant women should be counseled on nutritional needs and recommendations for optimal nutrition during pregnancy.

- Increase of 300 calories per day
- Daily prenatal vitamin, which includes folic acid 0.4 mg and iron 27 mg per day
- Avoid non-nutritional calories
- Abstain from alcohol
- Avoid tilefish, swordfish, king mackerel, and shark, which contain high levels of mercury
- Avoid unpasteurized milk and soft cheese and prepared and uncooked meats, poultry, and shellfish, which can contain the bacteria *Listeria*
- Limit caffeine to 200 mg per day

Exercise Counseling

- Review current pregnancy for contraindications to exercise
- Encourage exercise at least 5 days per week for 30 minutes
- Caution is warranted since increase in joint mobility can lead to injuries and falls
- Walking, swimming, cycling, and aerobic activity are good choices
- Downhill skiing, contact sports, scuba diving, and activities that could result in abdominal trauma should be avoided while pregnant
- Contraindications to aerobic exercise: hemodynamically significant heart disease, restrictive lung disease,

cervical insufficiency, multiple gestation high risk for preterm labor, ongoing vaginal bleeding in second or third trimester, placenta previa more than 26 weeks, preterm labor, ruptured membranes, preeclampsia

Vital Signs

Routine assessment of blood pressure (BP) and pulse are typically performed at each antepartum visit. Respirations and temperature are not routinely obtained without a medical indication. Women with illnesses, suspected fever, breathing difficulties, or other medical indications may warrant obtaining additional assessment data, including a pulse oximetry reading. Normal BP should be less than 120/80.

FAST FACTS in a NUTSHELL

It is essential to establish an accurate BP reading at the initial visit so that alterations in BP measurements can be quickly identified. Overweight women require a correctly sized cuff to avoid inaccurate readings.

Urine Sample

A urine sample is obtained at each visit and is dipped for protein and glucose. Ketones are occasionally measured but are not routinely obtained.

- Protein levels greater than 150 mg in nonpregnant adults are considered abnormal; however, in pregnancy, protein levels that exceed 300 mg are considered abnormal and require further assessment to identify possible etiologies. Protein is found in women with preeclampsia, kidney disease, and urinary tract infections. Other possible etiologies include renal disease secondary to other chronic medical conditions such as chronic hypertension and diabetes.

- Glucosuria can occur in pregnancy as a result of eating a high sugar meal, but can also be associated with gestational diabetes or unknown previous diabetes. While loss of glucose can occur in normal pregnancy, levels above 140 mg/day are considered abnormal and warrant further evaluation to determine etiological factors.
- Ketones occur when the body begins breaking down protein for fuel consumption and is typically associated with prolonged fasting, malnutrition, gestational diabetes, nausea and associated vomiting, poor eating habits, and insulin resistance.

FAST FACTS in a NUTSHELL

Abnormal urine findings warrant additional assessment to determine the causative factor. With proteinuria, assess BP and presence of leukocytes, which can be indicative of a urinary tract infection. With glucosuria, obtain a dietary intake history to determine if a high glucose meal or snack was recently consumed. If ketones are present, assess when the woman ate her last meal, presence of vomiting, and presence of symptoms associated with insulin resistance.

Review of Potential Warning Signs

The nurse asks the woman about possible warning signs that may indicate pregnancy complications. If any warning signs are identified, the nurse should immediately notify the practitioner. Warning signs that warrant immediate consultation include:

- Vaginal bleeding
- Uterine contractions more than 8 in 1 hour

- Amniotic fluid leakage
- Decreased or absent fetal movement
- Severe sudden headache
- Epigastric or right upper quadrant pain
- Urinary complaints such as oliguria or dysuria
- Sudden onset of edema, especially upper extremities and face
- Visions changes including blurred vision, double vision, presence of floaters in visual fields
- Vomiting longer than 24 hours
- Fever over 101°, chills

Determining Uterine Growth and Fetal Heart Tones

In the outpatient setting, the fundal height and fetal heart tones (FHTs) are typically obtained by the practitioner; however, in the inpatient setting, the nurse commonly performs this assessment. Once the actual gestational age has been determined, the nurse assesses the uterine size to see if it is within the expected range.

- The uterus should be 2 cm above or 2 cm below the expected uterine size. Uterine size is measured in centimeters with a measuring tape after 20 gestational weeks. Variations of 2 cm of expected uterine size can be indicative of possible complications with fetal growth or amniotic fluid volume and typically warrant additional assessment such as an ultrasound examination. The fundal height measurement guidelines are included in Chapter 2.
- Since most of the time the FHTs are heard in the lower quadrants of the abdomen, it is wise to begin to listen over those areas. In the third trimester, since most fetuses present in vertex presentation, the FHTs are also likely to be heard in this location, although they can be heard in various locations.

- The normal fetal heart rate (FHR) is 110 to 160 beats per minute (bpm). The FHR range should be documented along with the location at which the heart rate was heard. Any variations in the rate or rhythm require auscultation for a full minute. Abnormal sounds should immediately be reported to the practitioner.

ROUTINE SCREENINGS IN PREGNANCY

These routine screenings are offered to all pregnant women during the prenatal stage. Women with additional factors may warrant further testing and evaluation measures. The testing obtained at the initial pelvic exam is described in Chapter 2.

- Women from high-risk populations for contracting tuberculosis (TB) should undergo a routine purified protein derivative (PPD) test; high-risk populations include HIV-positive women, those living in crowded or institutional settings, those from countries where TB has a high prevalence rate and who immigrated within the last 5 years, those exposed to patients with TB, health care workers, or women with a history of intravenous drug use.
- Genetic screening serological testing needs are based on genetic history. In addition to those tests, routine serological testing performed at the initial prenatal visit typically includes:
  - Complete blood count
  - Hepatitis B
  - HIV testing (consent required)
  - Syphilis screening
  - Blood type and Rh factor
  - Varicella titer if varicella status unknown or thought to be negative
  - Rubella titer
  - Cystic fibrosis screening
  - Sickle cell screen if African American descent

Aneuploidy Screening

Aneuploidy screenings are aimed at identifying infants at risk for genetic disorders including trisomy 13, 18, and 21. Abnormal screening test results present the option for the woman to undergo diagnostic testing. Women with any known risk factors are given the option of diagnostic testing instead of screening methods.

Screening Methods

- First-trimester screening, which combines an ultrasound to evaluate nuchal translucency (NT) measurement, serum levels of pregnancy-associated plasma protein A (PAPP-A), free or total β-human chorionic gonadotropin (hCG), and serological maternal quadruple screening (maternal serum alpha-fetoprotein, hCG, unconjugated estriol, and inhibin A). Of these testing methods, the first-trimester NT combined test has the highest detection rate of all screening tests.
- Materni21 (circulating cell-free DNA), which is elevated in women who are carrying fetuses with specific genetic anomalies.

Stepwise Sequential Screening

- Combines first-trimester screening results (NT, PAPP-A) and second-trimester quadruple screening to determine risk of neural tube defects.

Diagnostic Testing

- Chorionic villus sampling (CVS) is a procedure where chorionic villi are removed from the placenta via needle aspiration for genetic testing. The procedure poses a very small risk of spontaneous abortion. CVS is generally considered higher risk than amniocentesis and cannot diagnose neural tube defects due to the early gestational age (10 to 13 weeks).
- Amniocentesis involves drawing a small amount of amniotic fluid from the uterus and confirms both genetic anomalies and neural tube defects. The test cannot be performed until later in the pregnancy (16 to 22 weeks).

TABLE 3.2 Ultrasound Use in Pregnancy

First-Trimester Indications	Second- and Third-Trimester Indications	Routine Review of Fetal and Maternal Anatomy (Performed After 18 Weeks)
Validation of intrauterine pregnancy	Gestational age	Brain anatomy (cerebellum, choroid plexus, cisterna magna, lateral cerebral ventricles, midline falx, cavum septi pellucidi)
Ectopic pregnancy	Fetal growth	Rule out any facial, palate/ lip abnormalities, position of fetal ears, head, and neck
Gestational dating	First-trimester aneuploidy screening	Evaluation of chest and fetal heart (four chambers, visualization of outflow tracts)
Evaluation of reproductive anatomy (cysts, fibroids)	Evaluation of complications (bleeding, pain, pelvic mass, uterine abnormality, size/date discrepancies, ectopic pregnancy, gestational trophoblastic disease, suspected placenta abnormality including previa or abruption, suspected amniotic fluid volume discrepancies)	Evaluation of fetal abdomen (stomach, kidneys, bladder, umbilical cord insertion into fetal abdomen and cord vessels number)
Identification of multiple gestation	Evaluation of fetal well-being	Evaluation of intact spine including cervical, thoracic, lumbar, and sacral regions
Identification of gestational trophoblastic disease	Follow up for abnormal conditions including abnormal biochemical marker results or congenital abnormalities	Extremities present with any abnormalities noted if possible
Confirmation of fetal viability	Determination of fetal position	Fetal sex (can sometimes be determined, only medically indicated in multiple gestations)
Evaluation of pain or bleeding	Assistance with invasive procedures (amniocentesis, cerclage placement)	Maternal assessment: uterus, ovaries, cervix, presence of any abnormalities, amniotic fluid volume, placenta position, grade, cord insertion site
Assistance with procedures (CVS, embryo transfer, removal of IUD)	Visualization of placenta location with external cephalic version	
Prenatal testing (nuchal translucency testing, early congenital anomaly identification)	Evaluation of fetal and maternal anatomy for late registrant for prenatal care	
	Serial examination of cervical length, funneling, and status of cerclage for cervical insufficiency	
	Rule out suspected fetal death	

Ultrasound Testing

Ultrasound is used for different reasons in various stages of pregnancy. Table 3.2 provides an overview of ultrasound testing in the different trimesters and in the detailed assessment that is performed in the second trimester to review fetal and maternal anatomy. Most women will undergo a second-trimester ultrasound; however, first- and third-trimester examinations are reserved for specific etiologies.

Screening Tests in the Second and Third Trimesters

The following screening is performed at 24 to 28 weeks:

- 1-hour glucose tolerance test
- Hemoglobin, hematocrit, and platelet count
- Antibody screening for Rh-negative women

Third-trimester testing performed at 36 weeks includes:

- Hemoglobin, hematocrit, and platelets
- Group *Streptococcus* culture

HEALTH PROMOTION AND RISK REDUCTION STRATEGIES

Multiple recommendations and considerations play a key role in establishing a healthy pregnancy. Women should be counseled on appropriate nutritional, environmental, and preventive health practices to reduce risk factors during pregnancy.

Nutritional Recommendations

- Focus on healthy weight gain, optimal nutrition, and incorporation of exercise.
- Counsel women not to eat undercooked meats, seafood, and unpasteurized dairy products. Certain fish should also be avoided. Limit caffeine to 200 mg per day.

Environmental Considerations

- Advise patients to discontinue cleaning litter boxes during pregnancy. If the woman must do this task, advise her to wear disposable gloves and discard them after each use. Women should also use gloves when doing yard work to avoid exposure to cat feces.
- Counsel women to avoid pesticides, insecticides, herbicides, fungicides, and other toxic chemicals.
- Discuss interventions to avoid elevated temperatures including fever, working outdoors in hot temperatures, hot tubs, hot baths, sauna use, and strenuous exercise.

Preventive Health Practices

- Encourage routine dental care and dental visits while pregnant.
- Stress the importance of continuing all prescribed medications including prenatal vitamins and iron.
- Discuss the need to report new physical symptoms or emotional changes that are concerning to the woman or her family.
- Review warning signs at each prenatal visit that warrant immediate reporting.
- Complete abstinence from alcohol, tobacco, and recreational drugs.

- Educate women to avoid individuals with fevers, rashes, or other illnesses.
- Encourage a flu shot for all pregnant women.
- Encourage attendance at childbirth education classes.
- Routinely screen for depression and domestic violence.
- Counsel on safe and appropriate seatbelt use in pregnancy.
- Counsel women on the need to avoid radiological examinations and to advise all other medical providers of her pregnancy especially when advising invasive treatments, radiological examinations, or use of medications in pregnancy.

COMMON DISCOMFORTS IN PREGNANCY

Pregnancy discomforts are commonly related to hormonal changes or mechanical changes related to the increased uterine and fetal size. Many symptoms in the first trimester are related to symptoms caused by hormonal changes. Table 3.3 lists common pregnancy discomforts that occur in the first trimester along with suggested interventions and underlying etiology.

Pregnancy discomforts that occur in the second and third trimester may be related to hormonal factors or the increasing size of the uterus and fetus. In general, the second trimester offers a break for many women from the symptoms of the first trimester that are related to hormonal influences as the body adjusts to the hormone elevations. Many women do not begin to develop unpleasant discomforts until the beginning of the third trimester. As the fetus grows and essential body structures are forced to shift into alternative positions, the woman may experience discomforts. Common discomforts, etiological factors, and suggested interventions are included in Table 3.4.

TABLE 3.3 Common Pregnancy Discomforts in the First Trimester

Discomfort	Causative Factor	Suggested Interventions
Breast changes/tenderness including increased size, feeling of fullness, tingling, nipple sensitivity, leaking of colostrum after 12 gestational weeks	Hormonal shifts with pregnancy	Wear a well-supporting bra. Some women may sleep in a jogging bra indefinitely during pregnancy. Avoid vigorous rubbing of the nipples with towels or clothing, or during sexual activity. Wear nursing pads to absorb colostrum if leaking is problematic
Constipation evidenced by dry, hard-to-pass stools, infrequent bowel movements, straining with bowel movements, and pain with bowel movements	Progesterone levels decrease gastric motility during pregnancy	Drink 8–10 glasses of fluid per day. Increase dietary intake of raw fruits and vegetables, and whole grain breads and pastas. Limit caffeine intake. Increase exercise. Stool softeners may be taken as needed
Nausea and vomiting	Elevated β-hCG levels	Eat small frequent meals, avoid hot and spicy foods, eat a high-protein snack before bedtime, limit fluids with meals but drink adequate fluid amounts between meals, avoid lying down immediately after eating, avoid strong smells that can increase nausea. Acupressure bands worn on the wrist, crystallized ginger, and camomile have been shown to be effective in reducing the severity. When nausea is associated with excessive vomiting, pharmacological intervention may be warranted (Phenergan, reglan, vistaril)

β-hCG, beta-human chorionic gonadotropin.

(continued)

TABLE 3.3 Common Pregnancy Discomforts in the First Trimester *(continued)*

Discomfort	Causative Factor	Suggested Interventions
Nasal congestion and epistaxis	Elevated progesterone levels	Blow nose cautiously and gently to avoid epistaxis, increase fluid intake, use cool mist humidifier in the home and when sleeping. Antihistamine for severe congestion, particularly when accompanied with a viral illness, can be used occasionally
Fatigue	Hormones	Ensure a full night's sleep (8 hours or more), adjust bed time as needed, frequent rest periods including daily naps as able, decrease fluid intake in the evening to prevent nocturia, always use good sleep hygiene measures (consistent time for retiring and waking up, avoiding caffeine in the evening, only using bed for sleep or sexual activity, avoiding stimulating activities in the evening)

TABLE 3.4 Common Pregnancy Discomforts in the Second and Third Trimester

Discomfort	Causative Factor	Suggested Interventions
Body aches (backache, sciatic nerve pain, abdominal pain, pelvic pain)	Increasing uterine/fetal size, loosening joints, lordosis caused from uterine/fetal size	Maintain proper posture, wear a pregnancy belt to decrease weight on pelvis, lie down on left side when possible with pillows supporting knees and ankles to assist with proper body alignment, positional changes, apply heat, Tylenol can be taken PRN (ibuprofen can be taken until 32 weeks), physical therapy intervention, chiropractor adjustments may be helpful, massage. Ensure abdominal pain is not related to uterine contractions
Sleep disturbances	Nocturia, frequent fetal movement, discomfort related to large uterine size, metabolism changes, leg cramps	Earlier bed times, frequent rest periods, empty bladder prior to retiring, limit fluid intake in evening, use pillows or pregnancy pillow for support of abdomen, back, and lower extremities when sleeping, proper sleep hygiene measures
Heartburn, indigestion, gastric reflux	Progesterone levels slow gastric system functioning and lead to inadequate closure of the esophagus, increased uterine size places pressure on gastric system structures	Eat slowly, limiting the amount of fluid ingested with meals and drinking adequate fluids between meals. Avoid greasy, high fat, spicy, and acidic foods such as juices. Avoid reclining immediately after meals and limit food intake prior to bed. Antacids can be used PRN. Zantac (ranitidine hydrochloride) is safe for use in pregnancy
Hemorrhoids	Progesterone levels decrease gastric mobility, constipation, enlargement of veins due to increased blood volume, uterine pressure on the rectum	Increase fluids and fiber-rich foods, avoid straining with bowel movements, comfort measures like sitz baths, witch hazel pads, fiber supplements (such as Metamucil, Citrucel, or FiberCon), and hydrocortisone creams and ointments

(continued)

TABLE 3.4 Common Pregnancy Discomforts in the Second and Third Trimester *(continued)*

Discomfort	Causative Factor	Suggested Interventions
Leg cramps	Changes in calcium processing in pregnancy	Stretch legs and calf muscles if spasm occurs, advise avoid pointing the toe but instead, advise dorsiflexing the foot toward the woman. Eat foods high in calcium, calcium supplements if diet is low in calcium, maintain exercise program in pregnancy
Itching, cholestasis of pregnancy	Hormonal factors, skin stretching, cholestasis of pregnancy	Use lotions or creams to keep skin moist, avoid extremely hot showers or baths, take cool baths, and avoid tight-fitting clothing with irritating materials. Cholestasis: routine liver function monitoring, ursodeoxycholic acid is used to treat severe itching and break down bile salts
Numbness or tingling in hands, carpel tunnel syndrome	Edema in hands and wrists	Take breaks from activities that involve extensive use of hands such as typing, knitting, or writing. Self-fitting splints are available in drugstores and can be worn for sleep or throughout the day as needed. Elevate hands when resting
Edema	Pressure of uterus and fetus, preeclampsia	Rest in a comfortable side-lying position with feet elevated when able; drink 8 to 10 glasses of decaffeinated liquids per day, limit salt in your diet. Wear support hose. Specialized support hose are available by prescription for women with varicosities, previous deep vein thrombosis, or peripheral vascular insufficiency
Varicose veins (hemorrhoids, vaginal varicosities, varicose veins in lower extremities)	Pressure of uterus decreases blood flow to lower extremities and return to the heart, increased blood volume increases vessel size	Avoid tight-fitting clothing including knee highs, elevate feet whenever possible. Lie in a left side-lying position when possible. May apply ice as a comfort measure. Be alert for onset of sudden pain, redness in a localized area, and positive Homans' sign
Urinary frequency and incontinence	Pressure from fetus pushing on bladder, urethra, and pelvic floor muscles. Severity increases with laughing, coughing, or sneezing	Empty bladder frequently, drink increased fluids to prevent dehydration, do Kegel exercises on a regular basis

PRN, as needed.

COUNSELING OPTIONS FOR LABOR AND BIRTH

Discussions regarding labor and birth should begin in the second trimester with open dialogue continuing until the birth, and should include:

- Birth plan with specific requests and preferences for the birth experience (intermittent fetal monitoring, ambulation in labor, labor or birth in water, avoidance of interventions, alternative positioning, children present at birth, involvement of partner or self in immediate postbirth newborn activities, placement of infant on maternal chest immediately at birth or handed to partner, ability to wear own clothes, nutritional preferences, discharge preferences)
- Exploration of feeding method with encouragement to breastfeed for 1 year
- Role of partner, family, nurse, doula, and practitioner during birth
- Preference for pain management strategies (natural, systemic medications, epidural)
- Opinions about induction, labor augmentation, and labor procedures (artificial rupture of membranes, fetal monitoring frequency, primary cesarean on demand)
- Newborn care procedures (vitamin K, erythromycin eye ointment, initial infant bath, hepatitis B vaccine)
- Cord clamping preferences and option for cord blood banking
- Newborn follow-up care needed, selection of pediatric provider with encouragement to meet with provider prior to birth
- Postpartum care issues (assistance at home, evaluation of support system, assessment for postpartum depression risk factors, birth control, returning to employment, breast pumping issues, sexuality concerns)
- Review of community support services: WIC (Women, Infant, and Child) programs, new mother support

groups (typically based in hospital or with county social services programs), postpartum depression support groups, lactation consultant services, early intervention services (if suspected delay or infant development concerns), health department or community clinics for newborn immunizations and ongoing pediatric care, parenting classes offered through county social services

4

Antepartum Preexisting Hematological and Cardiac Conditions

For the woman with a preexisting hematological or cardiac condition, pregnancy can be a time of great concern and stress about the woman's own health and that of her fetus. Appropriate management is essential for the nurse to provide ongoing assessment, treatment recommendations, ongoing monitoring, and patient teaching for the woman and her family.

After reading this chapter, the nurse will be able to:

1. Identify symptoms associated with iron deficiency anemia
2. Determine the appropriate plan of care for the woman with preexisting hypertension
3. Discuss the various cardiac conditions that can adversely affect pregnancy

EQUIPMENT

Blood pressure cuff, stethoscope, reflex hammer, urine dipsticks.

ANEMIA

Iron deficiency anemia affects 20% of pregnant women and it is most commonly associated with inadequate iron consumption in pregnancy and less commonly caused by HIV infection, blood hemoglobinopathies, and pica (i.e., when clay or starch is consumed, which results in malabsorption) (Candino & Hofmeyr, 2007).

Adverse Effects on Pregnancy

- Maternal depletion of iron
- Maternal susceptibility to infection
- Preterm labor
- Preeclampsia and eclampsia
- Iron deficiency anemia in infancy during the first year of life
- Stillbirth
- Neonatal death
- Low infant birth weight
- Postpartum hemorrhage
- Poor wound healing in the postpartum period

Treatment Recommendations

- Women with a hemoglobin level of less than 11 g/dL are treated with oral iron supplements of 60 mg/day.
  - While intramuscular and intravenous iron can be administered, they are reserved for severe anemia with hemoglobin levels less than 6 g/dL. Intravenous iron administration is associated with higher recovery of hemoglobin levels but also has an increased risk of venous thrombosis (Candio & Hofmeyr, 2007).

- Iron is more readily absorbed when vitamin C is taken concurrently. Women should be advised to take their iron supplement with orange, grapefruit, or tomato juice.
- The presence of calcium results in poor absorption, so women should avoid taking their iron supplement with antacids or foods high in calcium such as milk, yogurt, and cheese.
- Dietary recommendations should focus on increasing iron-rich foods such as organ meats, red meat, egg yolks, iron-fortified cereals, and legumes.
- Since iron can be constipating, some formulations contain a stool softener to decrease the incidence of straining, constipation, and hemorrhoids. Women should increase fluids and high-fiber foods to avoid constipation.

Monitoring Recommendations

- A complete blood count (CBC) or a hemoglobin and hematocrit level with a platelet count is typically performed at the initial prenatal visit.
- Mild or moderate anemia is typically treated with iron supplementation with a repeat test performed at 28 weeks and then again at 36 weeks.
- Women with severe anemia can be monitored after 4 weeks and should show marked improvement in hemoglobin levels.
- Women who do not show improvement warrant referral to a hematologist for additional iron studies and workup.

CHRONIC HYPERTENSION

Chronic hypertension is categorized as a blood pressure (BP) greater than 140/90 or currently on antihypertensive medications; this complicates 1% of pregnancies. Chronic hypertension is defined as increased BP before week 20 (or known to exist prior to pregnancy) or hypertension that is persistent for more than 12 weeks after pregnancy.

Adverse Effects on Pregnancy

- Carotid bruits
- Retinal changes
- Superimposed preeclampsia is a significant finding that may cause multiple complications including organ failure, hemolytic-uremic syndrome, thrombotic thrombocytopenic purpura, HELLP syndrome (hemolysis, elevated liver enzymes, and low platelet [count]), and disseminated intravascular coagulopathy.

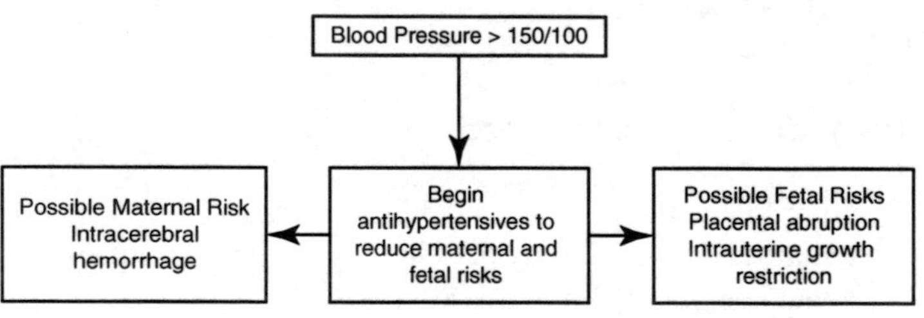

Treatment Recommendations

- Women with end-organ damage should begin antihypertensive therapy if BP exceeds 139/89.
- Preferred medications are methyldopa (Apo-Methyldopa) or nifedipine (Procardia), although other antihypertensives can be used. See Tables 4.1 and 4.2.
- Angiotensin-converting enzyme inhibitors and angiotensin II receptor blockers are *contraindicated* in pregnancy. Diuretics that are being prescribed prior to pregnancy can be continued; however, diuretics are generally not initiated in early pregnancy.
- Low-dose aspirin therapy (81 mg) is sometimes used and may result in a 15% reduction in the incidence of superimposed preeclampsia but has not been advocated

TABLE 4.1 Primary Antihypertensive Agents Used During Pregnancy

Medication Name and Dosage	Pregnancy Category	Mechanism	Maternal Side Effects	Neonatal Side Effects
Labetalol (Trandate) 200–2400 mg/day in two to three divided doses	D (in third trimester)	Alpha- and beta-adrenergic blockade	Tremulousness, flushing, headache, postural hypotension, bronchospasm	Decreased respirations in newborn
Methyldopa (Apo-Methyldopa) 0.5–3 g per day in two to three divided doses	B	False neurotransmission, central nervous system effect, reduces renal vascular resistance	Lethargy, fever, sedation, decreased mental acuity, sodium and water retention, hepatitis, hemolytic anemia, positive Coombs' test result, hepatic necrosis, granulocytopenia	None reported
Nifedipine (Procardia) 30–120 mg per day in slow-release preparation	C	Calcium channel blocker that blocks calcium ion influx across cell membrane	Orthostatic hypotension, headache, diarrhea, peripheral edema, dizziness, tachycardia	None reported

TABLE 4.2 Adjunctive Therapy Agents Used in Combination With Primary Antihypertensives

Adjunct Medication	Pregnancy Category	Maternal Side Effects	Neonatal Side Effects
Hydrochlorothiazide (Diurel) 12.5–50 mg per day	C	Initial decreased plasma volume and cardiac output. Electrolyte depletion, increase in serum uric acid, increased risk of thrombocytopenia, hemorrhagic pancreatitis	Thrombocytopenia
Hydralazine 50–300 mg per day in two to four divided doses	C	Initial decreased plasma volume and cardiac output	Thrombocytopenia

by national organizations as a standard of care (Carson, 2012).

- Recommendations for delivery
  - Vaginal birth is preferred with cesarean birth as obstetrically indicated
  - Women not requiring medication: 38 to 39 weeks
  - Women on medication: 37 to 39 weeks
  - Women with severe hypertension should undergo delivery at 36 to 37 weeks or once fetal lung maturity has been determined
  - Severe chronic hypertension with superimposed pre-eclampsia may warrant birth at 34 weeks or earlier if medically indicated

Monitoring Recommendations

- First-trimester baseline labs should include CBC count, electrolytes, blood, urea, nitrogen, creatinine, liver enzymes, urine or serum catecholamine concentration level, urine dip for protein, and a 24-hour urine collection for creatinine clearance and protein excretion
- Serial ultrasounds
- Repeat laboratory testing
- Office visits every other week from 24 weeks and then weekly after 30 weeks
- Nonstress testing should begin weekly at 32 weeks
- Co-management with perinatology and possibly with a hypertension subspecialist is encouraged

CONGENITAL CARDIAC CONDITIONS

Congenital heart defects complicate 1% of pregnancies. The risk in pregnancy is directly correlated to the specific defect, if surgical repair has occurred, and if any effects of organic heart disease persist. If the woman has had a repair with no adverse remaining cardiac effects, the risk in pregnancy is low.

Absolute Contraindications for Pregnancy

Certain conditions carry a contraindication for pregnancy since maternal death can occur in relation to increases in cardiac output, heart rate and blood volume. These include:

- Eisenmenger's syndrome
- Pulmonary hypertension
- Uncorrected coarctation of the aorta
- Severe symptomatic aortic stenois
- Marfan's syndrome with aortic root greater than 4 cm (Keane & Pyeritz, 2008)

Adverse Effects on Pregnancy

- Common cardiac conditions can impact pregnancy and warrant closer monitoring. Table 4.3 includes conditions, pathophysiological changes, and possible adverse outcomes that can occur in pregnancy.
- In addition, the Criteria Committee of the New York Heart Association has developed a classification system that outlines functional capacity related to ability to maintain normal physical activity (Table 4.4). Classes I and II are associated with positive pregnancy outcomes whereas Classes III and IV are associated with significant risks and adverse pregnancy outcomes (Table 4.4).
- Adverse effects depend on the condition, level of impairment created by the physiological changes associated with pregnancy, and the level of functioning that is possible in pregnancy. Any infection or anemia can worsen the prognosis since it increases cardiac output and warrants aggressive treatment.

TABLE 4.3 Commonly Occurring Cardiac Conditions and Effects on Pregnancy

Cardiac Condition	Pathophysiological Changes	Adverse Pregnancy Outcomes
Rheumatic fever	Inflammatory connective tissue disease often caused from group A beta hemolytic streptococcal infection, which can cause permanent heart damage and scar tissue formation on valves that can lead to stenosis and regurgitation	Risk of congestive heart failure due to increased cardiac output. Asymptomatic women also at risk
Mitral valve prolapse	Mitral valve leaflets prolapse in the left atrium during ventricular systole due to the thinning and elongated chordae tendineae, which are associated with a systolic click or, in more severe cases, a systolic murmur	Symptoms may include palpitations, chest pain, or dyspnea, which may be associated with arrhythmias
Peripartum cardiomyopathy	Dysfunction of the left ventricle that occurs in the last month of pregnancy or in the first 5 months after birth and associated with anemia and infection. Risk factors include advanced maternal age, grandmultiparity, and women of African descent	Symptoms include dyspnea, orthopnea, cough, fatigue, chest pain, edema, and palpitations. Congestive heart failure can occur. Subsequent pregnancy is contraindicated (Ladewig, 2013)

TABLE 4.4 New York Heart Association Functional Capacity Criteria for Cardiac Disorders

Functional Activity Class	Level of Functioning
Class I	Asymptomatic with no limitation in physical activity
Class II	Slight limitation in physical activity with no symptoms present at rest but symptoms occurring when some physical activity is performed
Class III	Marked limitation in physical activity. Comfortable at rest; however, symptoms occur with activity that is minimal
Class IV	Inability to carry on physical activity without discomfort. Symptoms of cardiac insufficiency or angina occur at rest and marked discomfort occurs if any physical activity is attempted

Treatment Recommendations

- Classes I and II are advised to undergo a spontaneous vaginal birth with pain relief in place and to reserve cesarean birth for obstetrical indications only.
- Classes III and IV may undergo labor induction with cardiac stabilization prior to induction. Close cardiac monitoring is warranted with invasive cardiac monitoring often indicated.
- Women should be provided with regional anesthesia to decrease maternal anxiety and maternal cardiac output.
- Limited pushing efforts are recommended with forceps or vacuum used to decrease maternal pushing since this increases stress on the heart.
- Office visits every 2 weeks and then weekly after 20 weeks of pregnancy.
- Any symptoms of cardiac decompensation warrant immediate hospitalization for stabilization with diligence between 28 and 30 weeks when blood volume peaks.

FAST FACTS in a NUTSHELL

Women with known cardiac conditions should consult a cardiologist and maternal–fetal medicine specialist prior to conception or in early pregnancy to develop a plan of care and determine level of risk associated with pregnancy.

- In labor, semi-Fowler's or side-lying position.
- Administration of recommended medications as needed for cardiac-related complications (Table 4.5).

TABLE 4.5 Common Medications Used to Treat Cardiac Disease in Pregnancy

Medication	Use in Pregnancy
Antibiotic therapy	Aggressive treatment of any infections
Heparin	Coagulation therapy
Thiazide diuretics or furosemide (Lasix)	Congestive heart failure
Digitalis glycosides	Cardiac failure
Quinidine	Cardiac arrhythmias

Monitoring Recommendations

- Ongoing collaborative management with cardiologist, maternal–fetal medicine, and obstetrical care provider
- Continuous fetal monitoring in labor
- Frequent labor assessments including maternal vital signs (maternal pulse greater than 100 beats per minute or respirations more than 24 immediately reported to obstetrical and anesthesia providers) and frequent lung auscultation for signs of congestive heart failure
- Close observation first 48 hours of postpartum period with frequent vital signs, semi-Fowler's positioning, slow gradual return to activity, stool softeners to prevent straining

5

Antepartum Preexisting Conditions: Infectious Diseases

For the woman with preexisting infectious disease, the potential of transmission to the fetus during pregnancy or during the birth process is a central concern during the antepartum period. Diligence in postpartum period is needed to prevent transmission of infection to the newborn.

After reading this chapter, the nurse will be able to:

1. Identify specific groups of women who warrant hepatitis B and C screening during pregnancy
2. Discuss appropriate treatment interventions for pregnant women who are HIV positive or who have AIDS
3. List opportunistic infections associated with HIV-positive infection
4. Discuss appropriate treatment interventions for the pregnant woman with a sexually transmitted infection (STI)
5. Discuss adverse outcomes associated with STIs during the antepartum period

EQUIPMENT

Cultures.

HEPATITIS B/C

Hepatitis B affects approximately 15,000 pregnant women and hepatitis C affects .15% to 2.4% of pregnant women annually in the United States (Centers for Disease Control and Prevention [CDC], 2013b). Risk factors for both include sexual transmission, exposure to contaminated blood products, and contamination of shared needles, which is common in intravenous substance abusers. Hepatitis B and C can both be passed from mother to fetus or during exposure during birth.

Adverse Effects on Pregnancy

In general, women with hepatitis do not develop an increase in liver involvement or a hastening of disease associated with pregnancy.

HEPATITIS B

- All pregnant women should undergo hepatitis B antigen testing in pregnancy.
- Women with new or ongoing risk factors for hepatitis B should undergo repeat testing upon admission to labor and delivery.
- If the mother is positive for hepatitis B surface antigen, the transmission rate to the fetus is 10% to 20%.
- If the mother is also positive for the hepatitis B surface antigen and hepatitis B e antigen (HbeAg), the transmission rate to the fetus is as high as 90%.
- If initial infection occurs during pregnancy, jaundice is more common.
- Acute fatty liver disease of pregnancy can occur due to the increased demands of pregnancy.

HEPATITIS C

- Women with risk factors should be tested for hepatitis C.
- Women with risk factors for hepatitis C should undergo screening in pregnancy. Ongoing risk factors or new risk factors warrant repeat testing upon admission to labor and delivery. Women with hepatitis C and HIV-positive status have perinatal transmission rates of 17% (CDC, 2013b).
- Transmission rate to the fetus is directly related to the maternal serum levels of quantitative RNA.
- RNA levels above 1 million copies/mL are associated with greater transmission rates.
- Greater transmission rates occur in women who are also HIV positive.
- Women with negative RNA levels do not transmit the virus.

Treatment Recommendations

Hepatitis B

- Women positive for hepatitis B should receive hepatitis B immune globulin during pregnancy.
- Infants with hepatitis B-positive mothers should receive the hepatitis B vaccine within 12 hours of birth, at 1 month, and at 6 months of age.
- All infants greater than 2,000 g should be vaccinated with the hepatitis B vaccine after birth prior to discharge.
- Encourage breastfeeding since it is not contraindicated in mothers with hepatitis B.

Hepatitis C

- Women with both hepatitis C and HIV should undergo an elective cesarean birth to reduce the transmission rate by 50% (CDC, 2013a). Elective cesarean section for women with hepatitis C alone is not a current recommendation.

- Avoid risk factors such as prolonged rupture of membranes for greater than 6 hours, perineal lacerations, and amniocentesis.
- Treatment with interferon is sometimes used in pregnancy and has not been associated with adverse fetal effects.
- Advise patients to avoid alcohol, Tylenol, and other drugs that can impair liver functioning.
- While breastfeeding is not contraindicated, women with cracked or bleeding nipples should refrain from nursing since hepatitis B can be transmitted via contact with blood.

Monitoring Recommendations

- Women with significant risk factors for hepatitis B should receive the hepatitis B vaccination during pregnancy with repeat HBsAg testing upon admission to labor and delivery.
- Baseline liver function studies should be obtained in the first trimester.
- Liver enzymes should be evaluated on a regular basis.
- Assess for upper quadrant pain since gallstones occur more commonly in women with hepatitis.

FAST FACTS in a NUTSHELL

Diligent handwashing is warranted after delivery to prevent transmission of specific infections.

HIV/AIDS

HIV infection occurs in approximately 6,400 pregnant women annually. Routine prenatal testing is recommended for all pregnant women (American College of Obstetricians and Gynecologists [ACOG], 2011). HIV infection is defined as the presence of the human immunodeficiency virus-1 or -2. AIDS includes all HIV-infected individuals with CD4 counts of fewer than 200 cells/mcL (or CD4 percentage less than 14%) as well as those with certain HIV-related conditions and symptoms.

Adverse Effects on Pregnancy

- Untreated women have a 25% risk of transmitting the virus to their fetus during pregnancy or at the time of birth.
- Women who are treated with antiviral therapy regimens have a 2% transmission risk.
- Increases in opportunistic infection often occur.
- Reduction in maternal immune functioning during pregnancy.

Treatment Recommendations

- HIV-positive women should be treated with antiviral therapy and zidovudine chemoprophylaxis during pregnancy to treat infection and prevent vertical transmission to the fetus.
- Plasma viral load determinations, CD4+ (cluster of differentiation 4), and T-lymphocyte counts should be performed at the initial prenatal visit as a baseline and every 3 months or after any changes in therapy have occurred.
- Antepartum, intrapartum, and neonatal antiretroviral prophylaxis should be administered.
- Scheduled cesarean delivery should be performed at 38 weeks before the onset of labor or rupture of membranes in women with viral loads greater than 1,000 copies/mL.
- If spontaneous labor or ruptured membranes have occurred, the use of cesarean section to decrease vertical transmission has not been established, so vaginal delivery can occur.
- Women with viral loads less than 1,000 copies/mL have a low risk of vertical transmission, so options for either route of birth can be provided.

- Breastfeeding is encouraged by the Centers for Disease Control and Prevention (2013a).
- Newborn treatment with antiretroviral drugs within 12 hours of birth is indicated in infants whose mothers are HIV positive.
- Infants born to HIV-positive women not taking an antiviral regimen or antiretroviral therapy before the onset of labor should receive a two-drug prophylaxis regimen.
- Administer routine newborn and infant vaccinations as indicated by current recommendations.

Monitoring Recommendations

- Newly diagnosed women should undergo baseline testing that includes CD4 count, HIV viral load, HIV antiretroviral resistance testing, hepatitis C virus antibody, HBsAg, complete blood count with platelet count, and baseline chemistries with liver function tests; these will be useful before prescribing antiretroviral prophylaxis (ACOG, 2013).
- Observe for opportunistic infections during pregnancy and treat accordingly (Table 5.1).
- Ultrasound screening is done at 18 to 20 weeks to screen for fetal anomalies.
- Any woman who develops an opportunistic pneumonia infection after 20 weeks is at an increased risk of preterm labor and birth and should be closely monitored for contractions.
- Women on newer drug regimens should have serial ultrasounds every 4 to 6 weeks to assess fetal growth and amniotic fluid volume.
- Counsel women to begin fetal movement counts at 28 weeks.
- If fetal growth lags or amniotic fluid abnormalities exist, fetal testing should begin at 32 weeks.
- Infants who are being treated with zidovudine therapy need to be screened for anemia at 2 to 4 weeks of age.

- Ongoing infant virologic testing with HIV-1 DNA or RNA assays should be performed initially at 14 to 21 days of life.
- If initial results are negative, repeat testing is done at 1 to 2 months of age and again at 4 to 6 months of age. Two positive test results indicate infection in the infant.
- Infants who remain negative at 12 to 18 months are considered HIV negative at that time.
- Infants who are positive on two occasions warrant referral to a pediatric HIV specialist.

FAST FACTS in a NUTSHELL

With the exception of HIV/AIDS infections and women undergoing treatment with antiretrovirals, women with other infectious diseases may safely breastfeed in the postpartum period (CDC, 2013a).

TABLE 5.1 Opportunistic Infections Related to HIV Infection

- *Pneumocystis jirovecii* (formerly *carinii*) pneumonia
- *Toxoplasma gondii* encephalitis
- Cryptosporidiosis
- Microsporidiosis
- *Mycobacterium tuberculosis* infection and disease
- Disseminated *Mycobacterium avium* complex disease
- Bacterial respiratory disease
- Bacterial enteric disease
- Bartonellosis
- Syphilis
- Mucocutaneous candidiasis
- Cryptococcosis
- Histoplasmosis
- Coccidioidomycosis
- Aspergillosis
- Cytomegalovirus disease
- Herpes simplex virus disease
- Human herpes virus type 6 (HHV-6) and type 7 (HHV-7) disease

(*continued*)

TABLE 5.1 Opportunistic Infections Related to HIV Infection *(continued)*

- Varicella zoster virus disease
- Human herpesvirus type 8 (HHV-8) disease
- Progressive multifocal leukoencephalopathy caused by JC (John Cunningham) virus infection
- Human papillomavirus disease
- Hepatitis C virus infection
- Hepatitis B virus infection
- Geographic opportunistic infections of special consideration, including malaria, *Penicilliosis marneffei*, leishmaniasis, isosporiasis, and Chagas' disease

Source: Kaplan et al. (2009).

FAST FACTS in a NUTSHELL

Any woman that develops one of the opportunistic infections during pregnancy should be rescreened for HIV if previously tested and had a negative test result.

SEXUALLY TRANSMITTED INFECTIONS

STIs are diagnosed in 19 million individuals in the United States annually and can result in maternal, fetal, or neonatal morbidity and mortality. Infection in pregnancy can be the result of preexisting infection prior to conception or can be contracted during the antepartum period (Table 5.2).

Adverse Effects on Pregnancy

- Spontaneous abortion
- Ectopic pregnancy
- Premature rupture of membranes
- Premature birth
- Stillbirth
- Neonatal infection
- Infant death

TABLE 5.2 Sexually Transmitted Infections (STIs) in Pregnancy and Recommended Treatment Interventions

STIs	Incidence in Pregnancy	Possible Pregnancy Implications	Recommended Treatment
Bacterial vaginosis	>1 million perinatal cases annually	Low birth weight, premature rupture of membranes, preterm birth, pelvic inflammatory disease (PID) can increase risk of ectopic pregnancy	Metronidazole 2 g in a single dose OR clindamycin
Herpes simplex	16.2% of population with 880,000 perinatal cases annually	Vertical transmission to fetus, transmission during birth process, neonatal herpes can lead to neonatal death, spontaneous abortion, premature birth	Acyclovir 400 mg orally twice a day OR famiciclovir 250 mg orally twice a day beginning at 36 weeks to reduce the incidence of an outbreak at the onset of labor; cesarean birth if outbreak occurs at the time of labor
Chlamydia	2.86 million cases annually with 100,000 perinatal cases. Most common STI in young adults under 25 years of age	Scarring can lead to PID and increased risk of ectopic pregnancy, preterm birth, neonatal infection (conjunctivitis, pneumonia)	Azithromycin 1 g orally in a single dose OR doxycycline 100 mg orally twice a day for 7 days

(*continued*)

TABLE 5.2 Sexually Transmitted Infections (STIs) in Pregnancy and Recommended Treatment Interventions (*continued*)

STIs	Incidence in Pregnancy	Possible Pregnancy Implications	Recommended Treatment
Gonorrhea	820,000 infections occur annually with 13,200 perinatal infections each year	PID can increase risk of ectopic pregnancy	Single intramuscular dose of ceftriaxone 250 mg PLUS either a single dose of azithromycin 1 g orally OR doxycycline 100 mg orally twice daily for 7 days
Trichomoniasis	1.09 million cases with 124,000 perinatal infections each year	Preterm birth, low birth weight	Metronidazole 2 g orally in a single dose OR tinidazole 2 g orally in a single dose
Syphillis	55,400 cases each year with 1,000 perinatal infections	Vertical transmission, low birth weight, premature birth, stillbirth, neonatal infection, infant death	Early latent syphilis: Benzathine penicillin G 2.4 million units IM in a single dose Late latent syphilis or latent syphilis of unknown duration: Benzathine penicillin G 7.2 million units total, administered as three doses of 2.4 million units IM each at 1-week intervals

IM, intramuscularly.

- Infection transmission to infant during birth
- Endometritis
- Neonatal infection
  - Conjunctivitis
  - Pneumonia
  - Neonatal sepsis
  - Neurologic damage
  - Blindness
  - Deafness
  - Acute hepatitis
  - Meningitis
  - Chronic liver disease
  - Cirrhosis

Treatment Recommendations

- Women with STIs should undergo education on safe sex and possible infection transmission to their babies.
- Positive results warrant immediate treatment and treatment of all sex partners.
- Women should abstain from intercourse until she and her partner have been treated and a test of cure culture has been obtained.
- Latex condoms should be encouraged to reduce the risk of infection during pregnancy.
- Expedited partner treatment is used in some areas and advocates for treatment of the partner based on a positive result without being seen by the woman's health care provider (CDC, 2006).

Monitoring Recommendations

- Screening for STI risk factors should be performed at the initial prenatal visit.
- Routine screening in pregnancy at the first prenatal visit should include chlamydia, gonorrhea, syphilis, hepatitis B, and HIV screening.

- Repeat screening upon admission to labor and delivery is advised for women with risk factors.
- Women who are at high risk for syphilis should be screened at the initial prenatal visit, 28 to 30 weeks, and upon admission to labor and delivery at the time of birth.
- Since reinfection is common, assessment for symptoms or repeat exposure should occur on an ongoing basis in pregnancy.

6

Antepartum Preexisting Neurological and Mental Health Conditions

Neurological and mental health conditions can adversely affect pregnancy and pregnancy outcomes. The most significant of these are epilepsy, mental health conditions, and substance abuse.

Epilepsy warrants close monitoring and ongoing neurological treatment during pregnancy. Uncontrolled seizures can result in fetal hypoxia and injuries due to falls. Medication exposure for the woman with epilepsy can put the fetus at an increased risk for certain birth defects.

Mental health conditions may worsen during pregnancy in response to hormonal influences and social stressors associated with pregnancy. Women with mental health conditions may need to discontinue certain medications completely or undergo medication changes due to potential teratogenicity.

Substance abuse is less common in women than in men but creates considerable risks for the developing fetus when used during the antepartum period. Certain substances can cause adverse maternal events, putting both the mother and fetus at significant risk in the antepartum period.

After reading this chapter, the nurse will be able to:

1. Identify the incidence and adverse outcomes associated with epilepsy during the antepartum period
2. Discuss the impact of certain medications used to treat epilepsy and the association with congenital malformations that occur when used during the antepartum period
3. Identify the incidence of specific mental health disorders that may occur during pregnancy
4. Define appropriate screening intervals for identification of mental health disorders in the antepartum period

EQUIPMENT

Culture collection tubes/swabs.

EPILEPSY

Epilepsy is a neurological disorder resulting in repeated seizures that often result in changes in attention or behavior (Engel, 2013). Epilepsy affects 0.3% to 0.7% of all pregnancies and is associated with a higher incidence of adverse pregnancy outcomes along with congenital malformations in infants born to epileptic mothers (Engel, 2013).

Adverse Effects on Pregnancy

Adverse effects on pregnancy are based on women treated with antiepilepsy drugs (AEDs) for seizure management. Women not on AEDs who are seizure-free do not have increased risk factors and adverse outcomes.

Adverse Maternal Outcomes

- Preeclampsia
- Gestational hypertension

- Bleeding in pregnancy
- Excessive bleeding postpartum
- Preterm labor prior to 34 weeks
- Reported increases in seizure activity range from 14% to 32% (Battino et al., 2013)
- Increased cesarean delivery rates

Adverse Fetal/Neonatal Outcomes

- Higher incidence of birth defects (3%–9%) related to the teratogenic effects of AEDs, which impair folic acid absorption (Battino et al., 2013)
  - Most common defects are neural tube defects, orofacial defects, alimentary tract atresia, diaphragmatic hernia, congenital heart abnormalities, craniosynostosis, and hypospadias (Battino et al., 2013)
- Childhood cognitive developmental delays
- Intrauterine growth restriction
- Low birth weight
- Neonatal bleeding if mothers are not given vitamin K injection at birth (1 mg intramuscularly is recommended)

Treatment Recommendations

- Avoid sudden discontinuation of medications in pregnancy, which is associated with sudden epilepsy-related maternal death.
- Counsel on the iMonitor serum AED blood levels obtained prior to pregnancy, then at least once per trimester (more frequently with Lamictal).
- Continue AEDs during labor.
- Counsel women that smoking when on AEDs increases the risk of preterm labor and birth.
- Monotherapy with low doses of second-generation AEDs is recommended (Table 6.1).
- First-generation AEDs are category D drugs and should be avoided in pregnancy (Table 6.2).

TABLE 6.1 Second-Generation Antiepileptic Drugs (AEDs) Pregnancy Category C
Lamotrigine (Lamictal)
Levetiracetam (Keppra)
Oxcarbazepine (Trileptal)
Topiramate (Topamax)
Zonisamide (Zonegran)

- Avoid use of combination therapy since this increases the risk of birth defects.
- Folic acid 5 g per day is prescribed for women on AEDs.
- Use of sodium valproate (Depacon) is associated with the highest incidence of birth defects, especially when dosages exceed 1,000 mg, and is not recommended in general pregnancy use.
- Lamotrigine has been identified as one of the treatments of choice; it has the fewest number of reported birth defects but results in reduced serum levels in pregnancy and can lead to breakthrough seizures.
- Carbamazepine (Tegretol) is often first-line treatment in pregnancy
- Vaginal birth is the preferred method of birth unless frequent seizures are present.
- If seizures occur in labor (2% to 4% incidence rate), intravenous phenytoin can be administered and birth via cesarean section is indicated.
- Seizures in labor increase the risk of placenta abruption.
- Encourage breastfeeding since AEDs are not a contraindication (Bangshaw, 2008).

TABLE 6.2 First-Generation AEDs: Pregnancy Category D
Valproate (Depakote)
Carbamazepine (Tegretol)
Phenytoin (Dilantin)
Phenobarbitol

Monitoring Recommendations

- Monitor for changes in seizure activity during pregnancy.
- Provide warning signs for women to call provider including onset of bleeding, premature contractions, and symptoms associated with preeclampsia.
- Co-management with a neurologist during pregnancy is recommended.
- Ultrasound at 18 to 20 weeks to identify potential congenital defects in the fetus.
- Intermittent ultrasounds to monitor fetal growth.
- Increase frequency of appointments after 28 weeks to monitor for pregnancy complications.
- Fetal surveillance during pregnancy should be initiated as needed for obstetrical complications or concerns.
- Observe closely in the first 24 hour after birth since seizure frequency increases during this time period.
- Women with ongoing seizure activity warrant seizure precautions during hospitalization.
- Teach safe infant handling for mothers in postpartum period to promote infant safety.

FAST FACTS in a NUTSHELL

While antiseizure medications can increase the risk of birth defects to fetuses, untreated seizures can result in significant hypoxia, making it more beneficial to utilize medication interventions than to leave seizure disorders untreated.

MENTAL HEALTH DISORDERS

It is estimated that 25% of Americans have some type of mental health disorder. Some mental illnesses are more common in women than in men. It is estimated that over 500,000 pregnant women (approximately 20%) have a preexisting mental health disorder. A mental health disorder is defined as any mental health disorder that affects mood, thinking, and behavior. Of those women with mental health diagnoses, one third will require pharmacological intervention during pregnancy (Davidson, 2012).

FAST FACTS in a NUTSHELL

Mental health disorders represent the most commonly occurring preexisting medical condition that occurs within the antepartum period.

Adverse Effects on Pregnancy

- Adverse effects on pregnancy are related to the specific condition as well as pharmacological interventions used to treat specific disorders (Table 6.3).

TABLE 6.3 Mental Health Disorders and Associated Pregnancy Outcomes

Mental Health Disorder	Incidence in Pregnancy	Adverse Pregnancy Outcomes
Depression	8.3%–16%	Preeclampsia, substance abuse, intrauterine growth restriction, low birth weight, preterm birth, childhood behavioral problems
Generalized Anxiety Disorder	9.5%	Spontaneous abortion, preterm birth, prolonged labor, increase in forceps births, nonreassuring fetal status, infant developmental delays
Obsessive-Compulsive Disorder	0.2%–3.5%	Spontaneous abortion, preterm birth, prolonged labor, increase in forceps births, nonreassuring fetal status, infant developmental delays
Posttraumatic Stress Disorder	2.3%–7.7%	Spontaneous abortion, preterm birth, prolonged labor, increase in forceps births, nonreassuring fetal status, infant developmental delays

(*continued*)

TABLE 6.3 Mental Health Disorders and Associated Pregnancy Outcomes *(continued)*

Mental Health Disorder	Incidence in Pregnancy	Adverse Pregnancy Outcomes
Social Anxiety Disorder/ Social Phobia	6.8%	Spontaneous abortion, preterm birth, prolonged labor, increase in forceps births, nonreassuring fetal status, infant developmental delays
Bipolar Disorders	0.5%–1.5%	Increases in symptomology during pregnancy, increases in psychiatric hospitalizations
Schizophrenia	.35%	Poor prenatal care compliance, smoking in pregnancy, premature birth, low birth weight, small for gestational age, increases in birth defects, stillbirth, infant death
Bulimia	0.2%–2%	Spontaneous abortion, breech presentation, twin gestation, nausea, preterm delivery, cesarean section birth, intrauterine growth restriction, premature birth, small for gestational age, low birth weight, smaller head circumference, low Apgar score, infant developmental delays, birth defects, cerebral palsy, increases in maternal smoking
Binge-Eating Disorder	4.1%	Excessive weight gain, maternal obesity, stillbirth, birth defects, macrosomia, cesarean section birth, increases in smoking
Substance Abuse	5%	Increased rates of HIV-positive, hepatitis, and sexually transmitted infections, poor compliance with prenatal care, neonatal withdrawal symptoms, placenta abruption, preterm birth, intrauterine growth restriction, fetal death, increased perinatal mortality, increases in sudden infant death syndrome, neurodevelopmental delays, behavioral issues, intellectual impairment, postpartum hemorrhage, preeclampsia, spontaneous abortion, congenital anomalies, fetal alcohol syndrome

Treatment Recommendations

- All pregnant women should be screened for mental health disorders or psychiatric symptoms at their first prenatal visit.
- A review of psychiatric medications should be performed as soon as pregnancy is confirmed. Women on category D drugs should be switched to safer drug regimens whenever possible.
- Multidisciplinary care with a psychiatric care provider is warranted during pregnancy.
- Support groups for pregnant women with mental health disorders or women with increased stressors in pregnancy, including online support groups, should be recommended.
- Women with substance abuse issues should be referred for detoxification and intensive substance abuse treatment.
- Pharmacological treatments may warrant adjustments during pregnancy and should be based on clinical symptoms.
- The use of pharmacological agents for specific treatment of various disorders is based on a risk versus benefit analysis, which should be performed by an experienced practitioner.

Monitoring Recommendations

- Women with risk factors for mental health disorders may warrant ongoing assessments for psychiatric symptoms during pregnancy.
- Suicidal ideations should be accessed since some disorders and pharmacological treatments increase the risk of suicide.
- Domestic violence and intimate partner violence are risk factors for mental illness and warrant assessment during pregnancy at the initial prenatal visit.

- Dual diagnosis (mental illness diagnosis and substance abuse disorder) should be assessed since 5% of pregnant women in the United States report illicit drug use during pregnancy.
- Women with substance abuse issues should be given routine drug screens during pregnancy.
- Women with eating disorders warrant monitoring by a nutritionist during pregnancy, close attention to weight gain patterns, and dietary recalls to assess nutritional adequacy during pregnancy.
- Antepartum fetal monitoring should be used when any growth abnormalities or other obstetrical indications are identified.
- More frequent prenatal visits may be helpful for monitoring symptoms and pharmacological effectiveness.
- Women with preexisting mental health disorders have a higher incidence of postpartum mood disorders and should be screened for postpartum depression and other psychiatric symptoms in the postpartum period.
- Maternal–infant attachment can be impaired in women with mental illness; therefore, close assessment is warranted. Referral to infant mental health services is often beneficial to this population.

7

Antepartum Chronic Respiratory, Metabolic, Endocrine, and Orthopedic Conditions

Chronic health conditions can potentially adversely impact pregnancy. Respiratory conditions need close monitoring to ensure the fetus remains properly oxygenized throughout the antepartum period. Because untreated metabolic abnormalities can result in substantial adverse fetal outcomes including fetal demise, early identification of abnormalities and tight control to regulate metabolic processes are imperative. Endocrine abnormalities can also lead to fetal loss and require close monitoring and management throughout the antepartum period. Some orthopedic disorders are treated with pharmacological agents that will need to be discontinued during pregnancy so immediate evaluation is needed as soon as a pregnancy is identified. The nurse plays an active role in early identification of preexisting disorders and appropriate teaching for the woman and her family.

After reading this chapter, the nurse will be able to:

1. Describe the symptoms associated with asthma
2. List medications that should be considered for the pregnant woman with asthma
3. Identify adverse fetal outcomes that occur with maternal phenylketonuria (PKU)
4. Compare and contrast pregnancy-related hyperthyroidism and hypothyroidism
5. List the appropriate screening intervals for diabetes detection during pregnancy
6. Describe appropriate diabetes management for the pregnant women with gestational diabetes or the woman with preexisting diabetes
7. Discuss the normal progression of rheumatoid arthritis that occurs during the antepartum period

EQUIPMENT

Inhaler, pulse oximeter, blood pressure cuff, glucometer and glucose test strips.

ASTHMA

Asthma is an obstructive lung disease that results in constriction of the airway caused by spasms of surrounding muscles, increases in mucus, and swelling of the airway walls due to the gathering of inflammatory cells. The incidence of asthma in pregnancy is 8% (Madappa, 2013). Of women with chronic asthma, one third will experience a worsening of symptoms in pregnancy with the most problematic period occurring between 24 and 36 weeks. Symptoms of asthma include wheezing, poor airway exchange, dyspnea, and coughing.

Adverse Effects on Pregnancy

- 10% experience an acute asthma attack while in labor (Madappa, 2013)
- Gestational hypertension
- Preeclampsia and eclampsia

- Premature birth
- Maternal death
- Stillbirth
- Fetal growth restriction
- Low birth weight
- Low Apgar scores

Prevention and Treatment Recommendations

- Consultation with a pulmonologist is recommended before pregnancy or in early pregnancy for women with moderate or severe asthma.
- Pulmonary function studies should be performed.
- Asthma triggers should be avoided. Common triggers include allergens (including pollen, mold, animals, feathers, house dust mites, and cockroaches), stress, and other environmental factors.
- Women with exercise-induced asthma should avoid strenuous exercise that is likely to trigger an asthma attack but should engage in walking and other forms of less strenuous exercise.
- Women should avoid individuals with infections and fevers since this is a common stressor.
- Medication adjustment to the safest profile possible is warranted. Preferred medications are presented in Table 7.1.

TABLE 7.1 Preferred Asthma Medications for Pregnant and Nursing Women

Bronchodilators	Inhaled Corticosteroids	Antihistamines	Decongestants (Nasal Sprays for Short-Term Use)
Short-acting	Pulmicort	Chlor-Trimeton	Afrin
Albuterol	Qvar	Benadryl	Neo-Synephrine
Long-acting	Flovent	Claritin	
Serevent Foradil	Aerobid	Zyrtec	
	Asmanex		
	Azmacort		
	Rhinocort (nasal spray)		

- Women with severe asthma may warrant oral or injectable corticosteroids, such as prednisone, prednisolone, or methylprednisolone during pregnancy.
- Short-term corticosteroids for severe asthma attacks can be used; however, increases in preeclampsia, premature deliveries, and low birth weight infants occur.
- Acute attacks warrant hospitalization with the administration of corticosteroids and high doses of oxygen, which are provided to maintain oxygen saturation levels above 95%. A beta-agonist with or without ipratropium is typically given for an acute attack.
- Sudafed was once commonly prescribed but is now contraindicated due to increases in abdominal wall defects in fetuses whose mothers took the medication.
- Allergen immunotherapy can continue to be used if already being prescribed prior to pregnancy. New therapy should be avoided in pregnancy.
- For women with severe and frequent asthma attacks, fetal assessment is warranted beginning at 32 weeks with nonstress testing on a weekly basis.
- Antibiotic use to treat infections in pregnancy should include penicillin, cephalosporins, and erythromycin.
- Annual influenza vaccination.

Monitoring Recommendations

- Women with moderate to severe asthma warrant ongoing care from a pulmonologist.
- Sequential medication prescribing is typically used with medications being added as needed for persistent or ongoing symptoms.
- If severe asthma attacks occur in labor, ongoing fetal monitoring is warranted since fetal hypoxia can occur.

DIABETES MELLITUS

Women with preexisting diabetes may have type I or type II diabetes prior to pregnancy. Normalization of blood sugars is key to maintaining a healthy pregnancy. Hyperglycemia during pregnancy is associated with complications and adverse fetal conditions. Diabetes occurs in 1% of all pregnancies with 90% of women having gestational diabetes (American College of Obstetricians and Gynecologists, 2005).

Adverse Effects on Pregnancy

Adverse effects directly related to the presence of hyperglycemia and diabetes include:

- Spontaneous abortion
- Stillbirth
- Macrosomia
- Congenital birth defects
- Difficult vaginal birth
- Traumatic birth injuries (brachial plexus injuries, fractured clavicles)
- Cesarean birth
- Preterm birth
- Hypoglycemia in neonate

Poorly controlled diabetes during pregnancy can also cause worsening of maternal symptoms including:

- Hypertension
- Preeclampsia
- Kidney disease
- Peripheral nerve damage
- Cardiac disease
- Blindness
- Increased risk of obesity and diabetes in later life

Treatment Recommendations

- Treatment is aimed at maintaining blood sugar levels at normal levels.

TABLE 7.2 Suggested Diabetes Treatment Recommendations for Pregnancy

Suggested Treatment	Specific Recommendations
Exercise	Exercise reduces excessive weight gain, increases optimal insulin regulation, and helps reduce the incidence of coexisting preeclampsia. Recommended exercise is 30 minutes per day most days of the week
Calorie consumption	Increased calorie requirements in pregnancy are based on maternal body weight. Women in normal weight range need an additional 30–35 kcal/kg/day. Women who are less than 90% of ideal weight should consume an additional 30–40 kcal/kg/day. Women greater than 120% of ideal body weight should consume an additional 24 kcal/kg/day during pregnancy.
Calorie meal distribution recommendations	Breakfast 10%–20% Lunch 20%–30% Dinner 30%–40% Snacks 30%
Insulin changes in insulin-dependent diabetic women	First trimester: Increased by 0.7–0.8 U/kg/d Second trimester: Increased by 0.8–1 U/kg/d Third trimester: Increased by 0.9–1.2 U/kg/d
Capillary blood sugar monitoring target levels	Fasting: <95 mg/dL Premeal levels: <100 mg/dL 1 hour postprandial: <140 mg/dL 2 hour postprandial: <120 mg/dL Overnight levels: >60 mg/dL Hemoglobin A1c concentration: <6%
Insulin selection	Short- or rapid-acting insulin prior to meals. Longer-acting insulin used for between meals and overnight. Intermediate-acting insulin is typically given before breakfast, with rapid- or short-acting insulin before the evening meal or at bedtime.
Hypoglycemia treatment	Hypoglycemia is more common in pregnancy, especially in type I diabetes. Levels below 60 mg/dL should be treated immediately with a glass of milk being preferable over juice. Glucagon should be kept on hand for severe hypoglycemia or loss of consciousness.

- Type II and gestational diabetes may be diet-controlled during pregnancy; however, type I diabetics typically are already being managed with insulin and will need to maintain insulin throughout pregnancy.
- Daily blood sugar monitoring is imperative and should include daily fasting blood sugars and 2-hour post-prandial blood sugars after meals. Table 7.2 includes treatment recommendations during pregnancy.

Monitoring Recommendations

- Close monitoring is essential so early identification and intervention for adverse risk factors can be reduced or prompt intervention can be initiated (Table 7.3).

TABLE 7.3 Monitoring Recommendations in Pregnancy

Monitoring Parameter	Specific Monitoring Requirements
Optical examination	Optical exam in first trimester and intermittent assessments if diabetic retinopathy is present.
Renal functioning studies	Baseline labs should include a 24-hour urine, serum creatinine, and assessment of urinary protein excretion (urine albumin-to-creatinine ratio or 24-hour albumin excretion) initially to assess renal functioning and then throughout pregnancy.
Antepartum risk screening	Ongoing assessment for common complications including preeclampsia, preterm labor, diabetic ketoacidosis, macrosomia, intrauterine growth restriction, hydramnios, congenital malformations, and intrauterine fetal death.
Fetal monitoring	Early dating ultrasound if no definite last menstrual period Ultrasound at 18–20 weeks Fetal echocardiogram if cardiac anomalies suspected Fetal movement counts beginning at 28 weeks Ultrasound as needed for size versus date discrepancies Nonstress test or biophysical profile beginning at 32–34 weeks either weekly or twice per week

(*continued*)

TABLE 7.3 Monitoring Recommendations in Pregnancy *(continued)*

Monitoring Parameter	Specific Monitoring Requirements
	Doppler velocimetry of the umbilical artery if vascular complications or intrauterine growth restriction is present.
Labor and delivery recommendations	Adequate glucose control: Deliver at 39–40 weeks Poor glucose control or previous history of stillbirth: Administer corticosteroids and consider amniocentesis 5 days later to determine lung maturity; when maturity of lungs established, proceed with delivery. Macrosomia with fetal weight estimated >4500 g: Consider delivery via cesarean route with lung maturity studies first if preterm. Monitor maternal blood sugar levels in labor since insulin needs often are reduced. Prepare for possible shoulder dystocia. Evaluate for cephalopelvic disproportion and need for cesarean section delivery. Delivery should be facilitated by 40 weeks since there is increased risk if pregnancy is prolonged.

FAST FACTS in a NUTSHELL

Of women who develop gestational diabetes mellitus in one pregnancy, two thirds will develop it in subsequent pregnancies, making weight loss prior to subsequent pregnancy, proper nutrition, and exercise important interventions for future pregnancies.

MATERNAL PHENYLKETONURIA (PKU)

Maternal phenylketonuria or PKU is an inherited condition where the body is missing the enzyme that is needed to break down the amino acid phenylalanine. If PKU levels build up, alterations in brain development and intellectual impairment can occur.

Adverse Effects on Pregnancy

- Women who are not following a strict PKU diet during pregnancy can develop maternal PKU, which can result in fetal abnormalities including microcephaly, intellectual impairment, behavioral problems, unusual facial characteristics (similar to fetal alcohol syndrome), and certain cardiac defects.
- Neurodevelopmental abnormalities are increased in infants whose mothers did not begin diet therapy during the first trimester.

Treatment Recommendations

- PKU levels should be below 6 mg/dL and can be reached through strict dietary interventions.
- Dietary changes include reducing foods high in phenylketonuria, such as meats, dairy products, and nuts.
- Advise women to increase low-protein foods such as certain grain products, fruits, and certain vegetables.

Monitoring Recommendations

- Referral for genetic counseling is indicated to determine fetal risk status.
- Women with PKU should have the father of the baby tested to determine risk of inheritance for the fetus.
- Targeted ultrasound at 18 to 20 weeks to determine if any fetal anomalies are present.
- Pediatric providers should be notified that the mother has PKU so ongoing neurodevelopmental screening can be obtained in early childhood.

- Ongoing monitoring by a nutritionist familiar with PKU is recommended.
- Diet recall diaries should be used to determine if adequate nutrition is being obtained.
- PKU levels should be obtained in the first trimester and be monitored throughout pregnancy.

THYROID DISORDERS

Thyroid disorders in pregnancy include hyperthyroidism or hypothyroidism. Hyperthyroidism is most commonly associated with Graves' disease, an autoimmune disorder. Hypothyroidism is more common in pregnancy and may be caused by Hashimoto's disease, an autoimmune disorder.

Adverse Effects on Pregnancy

Hyperthyroidism

- Maternal congestive heart failure
- Preeclampsia
- Thyroid storm
- Spontaneous abortion
- Premature birth
- Newborn complications
  - Tachycardia
  - Congestive heart failure
  - Premature closure of fontanels
  - Poor weight gain
  - Irritability
  - Compression of the trachea by enlarged thyroid
  - Low birth weight
  - Infant goiter

Hypothyroidism

- Spontaneous abortion
- Preeclampsia
- Anemia

- Congestive heart failure (rare)
- Fetal/neonatal complications
  - Low birth weight
  - Stillbirth

Treatment Recommendations

- Review for symptoms of thyroid disorders at first prenatal visit
  - Hyperthyroidism: Rapid and irregular heartbeat, a slight tremor, unexplained weight loss or failure to have normal pregnancy weight gain, and the severe nausea and vomiting associated with hyperemesis gravidarum.
  - Hypothyroidism: Extreme fatigue, cold intolerance, muscle cramps, constipation, and problems with memory or concentration. High levels of thyroid-stimulating hormone (TSH) and low levels of free T4 generally indicate hypothyroidism.
- Moderate to severe hyperthyroidism requires treatment with antithyroid medications. Use of radioactive iodine treatment is contraindicated.
- Methimazole (Tapazole, Northyx) is the most commonly used treatment but should not be used in the first trimester.
- First-trimester treatment with propylthiouracil is recommended
- Antithyroid medications can lower white blood cell counts and reduce resistance to infection; therefore, measures to prevent exposure to infections are warranted.
- Women on less than 20 mg of methimazole may breastfeed; however, higher dosage needs warrant formula feeding.
- Thyroxine is used to treat hypothyroidism but dosages often need to be increased during pregnancy in women with preexisting disease.
- Iodine requirement in pregnancy is 250 mcg, which can be obtained by using iodine-containing table salt.

Monitoring Recommendations

- Women with mild hyperthyroidism warrant monitoring but may not need treatment.
- TSH, T3, and T4 levels should be monitored monthly for hyperthyroidism and every 6 to 8 weeks for hypothyroidism.
- Liver impairment can occur with antithyroid medications so liver function tests should be monitored.
- Postpartum thyroiditis is a hyperthyroid state that is caused by leakage of thyroid hormones from an inflamed thyroid gland and lasts 1 to 2 months with subsequent hypothyroidism occurring for an additional 6 to 12 months. Any woman with symptoms should be screened in the postpartum period.

RHEUMATOID ARTHRITIS

Rheumatoid arthritis (RA) is a systemic autoimmune disease process that leads to swelling of the joints and other tissues as well as organ involvement. RA affects 0.5% to 1% of the population and is more common in women. Women with RA, just as with many of the autoimmune disorders, often experience improvement in symptoms during pregnancy; however, flare-ups in the postpartum period are common.

Adverse Effects on Pregnancy

- Women taking hydroxychloroquine for RA need an eye examination by an ophthalmologist to assess for drug toxicity.
- Nonsteroidal anti-inflammatory drugs should not be used in the first or third trimester. Third-trimester use is associated with premature closure of the ductus arteriosus, which can lead to fetal pulmonary hypertension.

- Use of corticosteroids may increase maternal hypertension, edema, gestational diabetes, osteoporosis, premature rupture of membranes, cleft palate, and small-for-gestational-age babies.
- Category X medications often used in RA include methotrexate and leflunomide, which should be discontinued 3 months prior to conception. Women who conceive on these agents should be referred to a maternal fetal medicine specialist to discuss possible fetal anomalies.
- Prematurity is increased.
- Small-for-gestational-age infants.
- Increased cesarean section rates.
- Recurrence of symptoms in postpartum period is common.

Treatment Recommendations

- Women with RA should have their medication regimens reviewed during early pregnancy to determine if any medications warrant discontinuation.
- Dietary recommendations include a low-fat, high-carbohydrate, high-fiber diet.
- Fish oil can improve symptoms and can be taken in moderate amounts during pregnancy.
- Vitamin D and calcium supplements should be encouraged.
- Smoking often exacerbates RA and should be strongly discouraged in pregnancy.
- Anemia should be treated with iron supplements upon detection.
- Folic acid supplementation of 0.4 mg per day is recommended.
- Regular exercise can reduce symptoms and is associated with improved pregnancy outcomes.
- Physical and occupational therapeutic interventions can improve symptoms and function.

- Breastfeeding, a hyperprolactinemia state, often increases flare-ups of RA and may be not be a viable option for some women with RA.

Monitoring Recommendations

- A functional assessment should be performed in symptomatic women to identify possible limitations related to the disease process.
- Anemia is more common in RA so complete blood count or hemoglobin and hematocrit monitoring during pregnancy is warranted.
- Prior to the birth, the provider should assess hip flexion capabilities. Limitations in flexion due to RA can impact labor and delivery and some positions may be painful, difficult, or impossible.
- If postpartum flare-ups occur, assess the woman's ability to lift and care for her infant safely.

8

First-Trimester Antepartum Complications

During the first trimester of pregnancy, considerable physiological changes occur. The majority of women progress through pregnancy without complications; however, some women will encounter pregnancy complications that occur as early as the first trimester. First-trimester bleeding is a cause for concern since it increases the risk of abortion, ectopic pregnancy, hydatidiform mole, preterm birth, and low birth weight fetuses. As many as 15% to 25% of all pregnant women experience first-trimester bleeding, with 50% resulting in complete resolution and experiencing no associated complications (Amirkhani et al., 2013). Some women experience severe nausea and vomiting during the first trimester that warrant aggressive management to prevent complications.

Perinatal infections that occur in the first trimester can result in spontaneous abortion while others can result in significant birth defects in the developing fetus. Although perinatal infections can occur at any time during pregnancy, most infections carry the highest risk when they occur during the first trimester when organogenesis is occurring.

Most surgical procedures and trauma/injury that occur in pregnancy are unplanned but thus create significant concerns for the health care team. Surgical interventions and trauma in pregnancy are included here, although they can occur at any time throughout the antepartum period.

After reading this chapter, the nurse will be able to:

1. Identify potential etiologies associated with various types of first-trimester bleeding
2. Describe appropriate interventions and strategies when caring for the woman diagnosed with hyperemesis gravidarum
3. Compare and contrast the different first-trimester perinatal infections and how they may impact the developing fetus
4. List the most common surgical procedures performed during pregnancy
5. Name the potential complications associated with trauma in pregnancy

EQUIPMENT

Sterile speculum, large vaginal swabs, ultrasound machine, culture tubes, Doppler.

BLEEDING ISSUES

Bleeding during pregnancy is not uncommon but results in considerable anxiety for the woman and her family. While some forms of bleeding are considered normal, others are worrisome. While as many as 25% of women experience some form of bleeding, 50% continue the pregnancy without complications. Bleeding during pregnancy warrants investigation to determine the etiology (Table 8.1).

TABLE 8.1 Types of Bleeding That Occur in the First Trimester

Type of Bleeding Problem	Incidence in Pregnancy	Signs and Symptoms	Nursing Interventions
Implantation bleeding	20%–25%	Light bleeding that occurs during the time when a normal menstrual cycle would start when the embryo is implanting into the uterine wall	Urine pregnancy testing to determine pregnancy status; if bleeding increases or continues, examination and serum testing are warranted; review for risk factors for ectopic pregnancy and previous pregnancy complications; provide reassurance
Bleeding related to intercourse	5%–6%	Bleeding occurs after sexual intercourse	Assess for any symptoms of infection; determine the amount, duration, and any associated symptoms such as cramping or clot formation; advise women to report repeated episodes; a pelvic evaluation can be performed if clinically indicated
Spontaneous abortion	15%–20%	Bleeding, may be normal to heavy; cramping may or may not be present; clot formation and heavy bleeding are associated with graver outcomes	Assess the amount, duration, continuation, presence of clots, heavy flow, and associated symptoms such as uterine cramping. For moderate to heavy bleeding, evaluation is warranted. Determine woman's Rh status since RhoGAM is often indicated if more than spotting has occurred

(*continued*)

TABLE 8.1 Types of Bleeding That Occur in the First Trimester *(continued)*

Type of Bleeding Problem	Incidence in Pregnancy	Signs and Symptoms	Nursing Interventions
Ectopic pregnancy	1.5%–2%	Unilateral abdominal pain or diffuse lower abdominal pain; spotting, fainting, dizziness; pain worsens and becomes more severe if rupture occurs	Assess for symptoms of pain, risk factors for ectopic pregnancy testing results, and presence of spotting. Medical emergency warrants prompt assessment since a ruptured ectopic pregnancy can be life-threatening. Early ectopic pregnancies may be managed using a protocol of methotrexate when no symptoms are present and hCG levels are less than 5000. Women with symptoms or higher hCG levels need surgical intervention. Women need hCG monitoring after treatment to ensure that treatment was successful. In women receiving methotrexate, if hCG levels do not fall, surgical intervention may still be needed
Hydatidiform molar pregnancy	0.75%	Uterine enlargement greater than expected for gestational age, vaginal bleeding, severe nausea and vomiting, first-trimester hypertension develops, absence of fetal heart tones	Assess blood pressure, nausea and vomiting, and vaginal bleeding. Provide order for ultrasound to confirm diagnosis. Once confirmed, a D&C (dilation and curettage) is needed. Monitoring of hCG levels are needed for the next 12 months to ensure early detection of malignancies. Conception is contraindicated for the next 12 months. Malignant gestational trophoblastic disease occurs in 20% of pregnancies (Davidson, Ladewig, & London, 2013)

hCG, human chorionic gonadotropin.

Adverse Effects on Pregnancy

- Pregnancy loss
- Maternal anxiety and stress
- Anemia
- Need for surgical intervention and possible general anesthesia
- Risk for alloimmunization

Spontaneous or threatened abortions during pregnancy can cause considerable concern. Determining the type of abortion provides the nurse with knowledge to provide patient teaching and prepare the woman and her family for possible clinical outcomes (Table 8.2).

TABLE 8.2 Classifications of Spontaneous Abortions

Type of Spontaneous Abortion	Clinical Physiological Findings	Nursing Interventions and Patient Teaching
Threatened abortion	Unexplained bleeding that persists for multiple days; cramping and a backache may be present. Cervix is closed upon exam	Provide teaching on reduction of activity, avoidance of heavy lifting and intercourse. Clinical outcome remains uncertain and ongoing bleeding is concerning. The absence of cervical dilatation is reassuring. Continued monitoring is warranted. Clinical evaluation to rule out molar or ectopic pregnancy is advised
Imminent/ inevitable abortion	Bleeding and cramping increase as bleeding continues, internal cervical os dilates, and membranes may rupture	Compassionate care is warranted as family is advised that the pregnancy will not continue. Options for immediate hospitalization for a dilation and curettage (D&C) can be discussed. If the woman

(continued)

TABLE 8.2 Classifications of Spontaneous Abortions *(continued)*

Type of Spontaneous Abortion	Clinical Physiological Findings	Nursing Interventions and Patient Teaching
		wishes to wait, careful monitoring for hemorrhage, anemia, and infection are warranted. Blood typing is done and RhoGAM is administered to all Rh-negative women
Incomplete abortion	Bleeding and cramping occurs and the cervical os is open. Part of the contents of conception have been expelled but a portion remains, which typically includes the placenta	Compassionate care to advise the woman the pregnancy has miscarried. Admission for D&C is preferable since hemorrhage, anemia, and infection can occur. Blood typing is done and RhoGAM is administered to all Rh-negative women.
Complete abortion	Bleeding and cramping may be active or may have previously occurred. The uterus is now empty and may be contracted and contains no products of conception. The cervical os may be closing or already be closed	Advise the woman the fetus is no longer present. Determine blood type and Rh status to determine if it is still feasible to give RhoGAM if within 72 hours of the onset of bleeding. Counsel Rh-negative women on the importance of RhoGAM administration following a pregnancy loss. Encourage abstinence until follow-up physical examination is performed. Contraception is recommended until regular menstrual cycles occur
Missed abortion	Fetal death occurs in utero; however, bleeding and cramping do not occur. Uterine growth stops, breast changes typically cease, and brownish vaginal bleeding may occur	If unable to obtain fetal heart tones in a pregnancy that should be 12 weeks or if size of uterus is less than dates, obtain an ultrasound. If fetal death is anticipated to

(continued)

TABLE 8.2 Classifications of Spontaneous Abortions *(continued)*

Type of Spontaneous Abortion	Clinical Physiological Findings	Nursing Interventions and Patient Teaching
		have occurred >4 weeks, obtain coagulation studies since disseminated intravascular coagulation (DIC) can occur. Counsel woman that loss has occurred. If <10 weeks gestational size, misoprostol can be used to perform a medical (nonsurgical) abortion. If >10 gestational weeks, schedule a D&C. RhoGAM is warranted for all Rh-negative women.
Recurrent pregnancy loss	Abortion occurs in 3 or more consecutive pregnancies	Testing should be performed including thyroid function tests, thyroid antibodies, diabetes screening, hormone levels to assess ovarian reserve, antiphospholipid syndrome, inherited thrombophilias, and abnormal parental karyotypes
Septic abortion	Infection that occurs when bacteria enter the uterine cavity. May be related to sexually transmitted infections, prolonged unrecognized rupture of membranes, pregnancy with an IUD in place, or in rare cases attempts by the woman to self-terminate the pregnancy or a failed elective abortion that was done inadequately	Prompt intervention is warranted via D&C or misoprostol since untreated septic abortion can result in septic shock and septicemia. Intravenous broad-spectrum antibiotics should be given

Women with a missed abortion or an imminent abortion may wish to consider undergoing treatment with a medical (nonsurgical) abortion as a means of avoiding surgical intervention and general anesthesia. Women should be counseled that some attempts at medical abortion may be unsuccessful making surgical intervention necessary.

Medical (Nonsurgical) Abortion Procedure for Missed Abortion

1. Determine estimated gestational age and document absence of fetal heart tones.
2. Obtain ultrasound to determine gestational size of pregnancy and confirm fetal demise and absence of fetal heart activity. Confirm intrauterine pregnancy and document that ectopic pregnancy has been excluded.
3. Document that pregnancy is less than 10 weeks gestational size. Pregnancies greater than 10 weeks gestational size are excluded from a medical abortion.
4. Obtain Rh screen, hematocrit, and quantitative serum hCG
5. Provide patient teaching on signs of hemorrhage or other complications that warrant emergency intervention; that is, more than 2 pads per hour vaginal bleeding
6. Pain medication is provided. Either ibuprofen 800 mg every 6 to 8 hours or Tylenol #3 every 4 to 6 hours is given.
7. Clinician inserts 800 mcg misoprostol vaginally and patient is sent home
8. If bleeding is not heavier than a period, or if no products of conception are passed within 12 to14 hours, a repeat dose of 800 mcg is administered.
9. If repeat dose does not result in passage of products of conception, a D&C is necessary.
10. Follow-up care includes either a quantitative hCG level, which should fall by at least 50% from the previous documented level, or an ultrasound transvaginal examination that reveals an empty uterus.
11. The woman returns for a physical examination at 2 weeks after the procedure.
12. Patient should refrain from intercourse until follow-up exam is completed.
13. RhoGAM is administered to Rh-negative women.
14. Women wishing to become pregnant in the near future should continue prenatal vitamins.

FAST FACTS in a NUTSHELL

When a woman is experiencing vaginal bleeding, if the blood is expelled into the toilet and the amount seems considerable upon inspection, advise the woman to wear a sanitary pad and keep track of bleeding by the number of saturated pads she uses. It is important to note the size of the pad and differentiate between a panty liner verses a large overnight pad to determine variations in bleeding that is being reported.

HYPEREMESIS GRAVIDARUM

Hyperemesis gravidarum consists of prolonged nausea and vomiting that often result in ketosis and a weight loss of more than 5% of maternal pre-pregnancy weight. The incidence is 0.3% to 2% in the United States (Ladewig et al., 2014).

Adverse Effects on Pregnancy

- Dehydration
- Electrolytes and acid–base imbalances
- Nutritional deficiencies
- Profound maternal weight loss
- Maternal functional impairment
- Maternal death (rare)
- Low birth weight
- Small for gestational age
- Preterm birth
- Low 5-minute Apgar scores less than 7

Treatment Recommendations

- Pharmacological treatment of hyperthyroidism if identified as causative factor

- Offer counseling resources (50% experience relationship issues as a result of strained marital relationships due to disorder) (Ogunyemi, 2011).
- Consider alternative therapies as needed (acupressure, hypnosis, crystalized ginger capsules 250 mg four times a day)
- Vitamin B_6 (10–25 mg three times a day)
- Psychological counseling, antidepressant and cognitive behavioral therapy as needed
- Intravenous hydration (home or inpatient) as needed
- Dietary recommendations
    - Small frequent bland meals when hungry, with crackers in the morning
    - High-protein snacks
    - Limit iron supplements, which worsen symptoms
    - Herbal teas (peppermint or ginger, other ginger-containing beverages)
    - Broth
    - Dry toast
    - Gelatin
    - Popsicles
- Pharmacological treatment options
    - Doxylamine (Unisom) 12.5 mg three or four times a day
    - Metoclopramide (Reglan) 5–10 mg taken orally every 8 hours
    - Promethazine (Phenergan) 12.5 mg orally or rectally every 4 hours
    - Dimenhydrinate (Benedryl) 50–100 mg orally every 4 to 6 hours as needed
    - Methylprednisolone (Medrol) 16 mg orally or IV every 8 hours for 3 days (contraindicated first trimester)
    - Parental potassium if hypokalemia is severe or symptomatic to achieve a concentration of 40 mEq/L (and not greater than 80 mEq/L) with infusion rate of 10 mEq of potassium/hr with ongoing assessment of urine output
    - Total parenteral nutrition or nasogastric tube feeding as needed

TABLE 8.3 Suggested Laboratory Studies for Women With Hyperemesis Gravidarum

Urinalysis
Serum electrolyte and ketones
Liver enzymes and bilirubin
Amylase/lipase
Thyroid-stimulating hormone, free thyroxine
Urine culture
Calcium levels
Serum *Helicobacter pylori* antibody panel
Hematocrit
Hepatitis panel
First-trimester diabetes screening
Ultrasound to detect molar pregnancy or multiple gestation
Abdominal ultrasound to evaluate pancreas and/or biliary tree as needed

Monitoring Recommendations

- Suggested laboratory studies should be performed initially and as needed (Table 8.3)
- Careful vital signs assessment at each visit including standing and lying blood pressure and pulse
- Assess volume status (mucous membrane condition, skin turgor, neck vein distension, mental status)
- Assess for presence of associated symptoms (Table 8.4)
- Depression screening during pregnancy
- Dietary recall and ongoing nutrition consult

TABLE 8.4 Common Associated Symptoms of Hyperemesis Gravidarum

Ptyalism (excessive salivation)
Fatigue
Weakness
Dizziness
Sleep disturbance
Hyperolfaction
Dysgeusia
Decreased gustatory discernment
Depression
Anxiety
Irritability
Mood changes
Decreased concentration

FAST FACTS in a NUTSHELL

Due to cost considerations for certain medications, some insurance companies may limit the amount of allowable pills per prescription or month. Women who need quantities higher than allowable amounts will need letters of medical necessity completed and submitted to the insurance company to ensure the woman is receiving an adequate quantity to control her symptoms.

PERINATAL INFECTION

Certain perinatal infections occurring in pregnancy can cause adverse fetal effects. Exposure in the first trimester can cause fetal defects while later exposure can cause growth alterations, preterm birth, or neurodevelopmental issues in the newborn.

Adverse Effects on Pregnancy

Specific alterations or defects are directly correlated with the type of infection and when in the pregnancy it occurs. Table 8.5 includes commonly occurring infections, timing of exposure with greatest adverse effects, specific adverse fetal effects that can occur, and recommended treatment measures.

Treatment Recommendations

- The specific treatment approaches are based on the type of infection (Table 8.5).
- If infection is contracted during pregnancy, household contacts should be vaccinated when a vaccine is available.

TABLE 8.3 Common Infections That [illegible] in Pregnancy

Type of Infection	Timing of Exposure With Greatest Adverse Effects	Types of Fetal Effects Associated With Infection	Recommended Treatment During Pregnancy
Cytomegalovirus (CMV)	First-trimester greatest risk (1 in 3 risk of fetal infection). Women with chronic CMV have a 1% risk of fetal infection	Intrauterine growth restriction Small for gestational age Hydramnios Fetal hydrops Cardiomegaly Fetal ascites Microcephaly Hydrocephaly Intellectual disability Cerebral palsy Newborn jaundice Seizures Neurological impairment	No treatment exists during pregnancy. Infant screening after 3 weeks of birth (earlier testing will yield maternal status and should not be performed). If known exposure, antepartum fetal surveillance and serial ultrasound screening are warranted. Limited data on use of ganciclovir have shown improvement in neurodevelopmental and hearing impairment but it is considered experimental due to adverse side effects (Centers for Disease Control and Prevention [CDC], 2010)
Group beta streptococcal infection	Can be vertical transmission during pregnancy or exposure at time of birth	Pneumonia Apnea Shock Meningits Neurodevelopmental abnormalities Death	If the mother is positive on culture, then treat in labor with penicillin G 5 million units IV, then 2.5–3 million units every 4 hours until birth. If penicillin PCN allergy, clindamycin 900 mg IV every 4 hours if susceptible. If not, then vancomycin 1 g every 12 hours until birth
Human parovirus 19	Infection before 20 weeks has greatest risk	Spontaneous abortion Fetal anemia Fetal hydrops	Doppler studies weekly if known exposure occurs in pregnancy Fetal transfusion for severe anemia

(continued)

TABLE 8.5 Common Infections That Occur in Pregnancy *(continued)*

Type of Infection	Timing of Exposure With Greatest Adverse Effects	Types of Fetal Effects Associated With Infection	Recommended Treatment During Pregnancy
		Stillbirth Neonatal death	Ultrasound assessment weekly to assess for hydrops
Listeria monocytogenes	Adverse effects if contracted during pregnancy. Third trimester has highest incidence of infection	Spontaneous abortion Premature birth Stillbirth or neonatal death rate is 20%–22% (Weinstein, 2012)	Ampilcillin or penicillin IV Serial ultrasounds to assess fetal well-being
Lymphocytic choriomeningitis virus	Adverse effects if contracted during pregnancy	Spontaneous abortion Birth defects Neonatal infection Stillbirth	No treatment
Rubella	First-trimester infection causes congenital rubella infection in fetuses	Blindness Congenital cataracts Deafness Congenital heart defects Cerebral palsy Intellectual impairment Infant remains infectious for months after birth	Test for rubella immunity at first prenatal visit Avoid exposure to unvaccinated individuals during pregnancy If infection is suspected, laboratory testing should be performed. IgM antibodies might not be detectable before 4–5 days after rash onset. If negative, rubella IgM and IgG results are obtained from specimens taken before 4–5 days, repeat lab testing. No pharmacological intervention is available. Determination of exact gestational age at time of exposure is crucial. Some women with first-trimester exposure may consider elective termination

TABLE 8.5 Common Infections That Occur in Pregnancy *(continued)*

Type of Infection	Timing of Exposure With Greatest Adverse Effects	Types of Fetal Effects Associated With Infection	Recommended Treatment During Pregnancy
Toxoplasmosis	First-trimester exposure yields highest adverse effects but fetal infection rates are highest in last month of pregnancy. If mother previously exposed PRIOR to pregnancy, no risks since infant will then have immunity	Retinochoriditis (mild cases) Spontaneous abortion Fetal ascites Intracranial calcifications Intrauterine growth restriction Seizures Coma Microcephaly Hydrocephalus Blindness Deafness Intellectual impairment Stillbirth Infant death Other signs may not occur until adulthood in individuals affected at birth	Spiramycin (first and early second trimesters) or pyrimethamine/sulfadiazine and leucovorin (for late second and third trimesters) Congenitally infected newborns pyrimethamine, a sulfonamide, and leucovorin for 1 year (CDC, 2013c)
Varicella	First-trimester infection can result in congenital varicella syndrome (0.4%–2%). Exposure 5 days prior to delivery to 2 days after birth can cause newborn infection	Low birth weight Skin scarring Newborn infection at birth has 30% fatality rate	No treatment If elective cesarean is scheduled, delay birth if possible to decrease infection incidence in newborn

Monitoring Recommendations

- Most prenatal exposures will warrant ongoing fetal surveillance in pregnancy (Table 8.5).

SURGERY DURING PREGNANCY

Surgery during pregnancy is rarely performed (0.75% of all pregnancies; Ladewig et al., 2014). The most common surgical procedures during pregnancy include: appendicitis, biliary disease, and ovarian cysts. Trauma in pregnancy is associated with motor vehicle accidents, falls, and domestic violence and affects 3% to 8% of pregnancies.

Adverse Effects on Pregnancy

- Preterm labor
- Nonreassuring fetal status
- Maternal respiratory depression
- Pneumonia
- Thrombophlebitis
- Fetal injury
- Fetal death

Treatment Recommendations

- Utilize ultrasound for diagnosis whenever possible.
- CT scan without contrast and MRI deliver a low radiation dose and can be used as needed.
- Laparoscopy procedures are preferred whenever possible.
- Left lateral tilt positioning during surgery is indicated.
- Ovarian masses greater than 6 cm, those that are symptomatic, ovarian torsion, or malignancies warrant surgical intervention; laparoscopy is preferred.
- Obstetrical consult for all surgery patients.

- If preterm labor occurs during surgery, administer tocolytics.
- Consider nasogastric tube for major abdominal surgery.
- Sequential compression stockings postoperatively
- Encourage turn, cough, deep breathing, leg exercises, and early ambulation.

Monitoring Recommendations

- Ovarian masses less than 6 cm may be monitored.
- Fetal heart rate monitoring pre- and postoperatively is warranted.
- Monitor for maternal hypoxia and fetal bradycardia during surgery.
- Assess lung sounds, Homans' sign, bowel sounds, fetal movement, and fetal heart rate.

TRAUMA/INJURY DURING PREGNANCY

Trauma occurs in 6% to 7% of pregnant women (Davidson et al., 2013). Motor vehicle accidents are the most common cause with domestic violence and falls also highly prevalent.

Adverse Effects on Pregnancy

- Vaginal bleeding
- Preterm labor
- Rupture of membranes
- Placental abruption
- Fetomaternal hemorrhage
- Fetal injury
- Fetal death
- Uterine rupture
- Shock

Treatment Recommendations

- Ensure airway and cervical spine stability
- Breathing and circulation management
- Supplemental oxygen
- Left lateral tilt for patients greater than 20 weeks
- Administer RhoGAM if fetomaternal bleed; if fetal cells are greater than 30 mL, additional RhoGAM is indicated
- If CPR is unsuccessful in the first 3 to 4 minutes and gestational age is more than 24 to 25 weeks, perform perimortem cesarean birth
- Victims of violence should be referred for counseling and given written resources, support group information, and shelter locations and contact information

Monitoring Recommendations

- Kleihauer-Betke testing if greater than 16 weeks with repeat in 24 hours
- Continuous electronic fetal monitoring
- Radiological studies with screening of abdomen from radiation
- Abdominal gunshot wounds will require radiological studies
- Obstetric ultrasound
- Tocolytics for preterm labor or onset of uterine contractions
- Biophysical profile if third-trimester injury
- If abuse is disclosed as the causative factor, follow-up warrants referrals to resources

FAST FACTS in a NUTSHELL

Women are more likely to be abused during pregnancy than any other time in their lives. Ongoing assessment for intimate partner violence is essential to ensure that abused women are properly identified, since many will not readily admit to being abused when initially asked. Women are more likely to disclose abuse to an individual they trust and with whom they have an established relationship.

9

Second- and Third-Trimester Complications

Pregnancy complications can occur at any time during the antepartum period. Second-trimester pregnancy complications may include cervical insufficiency, which puts the fetus at risk for fetal loss or preterm birth. Multiple gestations carry increased risks and warrant ongoing assessment to detect early indicators of complications.

Placental and cord insertion problems are usually detected during routine ultrasound, which is performed between 18 and 20 gestational weeks. Women who experience premature rupture of membranes or preterm labor are at risk for preterm birth, which carries considerable risk for the premature newborn. Ongoing nursing assessments can identify complications early and enable the medical team to intervene to improve perinatal outcomes.

After reading this chapter, the nurse will be able to:

1. Identify women at risk for cervical insufficiency
2. Describe patient education for the woman undergoing a cervical cerclage for cervical insufficiency

3. List interventions for women with a multiple gestation aimed at reducing the risk of preterm birth
4. List the different types of placental and cord insertion abnormalities and the recommended approaches to reduce adverse outcomes
5. Define the approach to care management for the woman with premature rupture of membranes
6. Discuss strategies for the care of the woman with preterm labor to reduce the likelihood of a preterm birth

EQUIPMENT

Sterile speculum, light source for pelvic examination, ultrasound machine, glass slides, cultures, cotton swabs, nitrazine paper, electronic fetal monitor, intravenous fluids and tubing.

CERVICAL INSUFFICIENCY

Cervical insufficiency (CI) occurs when painless cervical dilation results in recurrent second-trimester pregnancy losses or births in otherwise normal pregnancies, or when structural weakness of the cervical tissue occurs. CI can also be defined by the presence of a transvaginal cervical length less than 25 mm and/or advanced cervical changes on physical examination before 24 weeks of gestation. CI can either be congenital or acquired.

Adverse Effects on Pregnancy

- Second-trimester pregnancy loss
- Preterm birth

Treatment Recommendations

- A complete assessment for risk factors associated with congenital or acquired CI:
  - Collagen abnormalities
  - Uterine defects
  - Diethylstilbestrol (DES) exposure

  - Ultrasound finding of a cervix less than 25 mm in length
  - Obstetrical trauma in the past
  - Past mechanical dilatation
  - Treatment of cervical intraepithelial neoplasia
  - Physical exam findings of cervical softening
  - Suprapubic or fundal pressure or Valsalva maneuver that reveals membranes in the endocervical canal or vagina
  - Maternal symptoms of pelvic pressure, premenstrual-like cramping or backache, and increased vaginal discharge
- Preventive cerclage placement at 12 to 14 weeks if clinically indicated
- Progesterone supplementation from 16 to 36 weeks
- Abdominal cerclage may be considered for a previous failed cervical cerclage
- Advise against intercourse when risk factors are identified or cerclage is in place

Monitoring Recommendations

- Cervical length screening at 14 weeks for all women with a prior preterm birth or pregnancy loss
- Cervical length screening for all women with risk factors who are nulliparous or those who have no history of loss or preterm birth at 18 to 24 weeks
- Once placed, assess cerclage to ensure it is intact and no bleeding is noted
- Preterm cerclage removal is indicated if labor ensues that cannot be stopped, or if bleeding, nonreassuring fetal status, or membrane rupture occurs

FETAL DEMISE

Fetal demise is typically classified as a fetal loss that occurs after 20 weeks, although in some states, any nonlive birth in which the fetus weighs more than 350 g regardless of gestational age also fits this category. In the United States, the rate of stillbirth is 6.2 per 1,000 births.

Adverse Effects on Pregnancy

- Significant psychological effects
- Significant family grief
- Maternal coagulopathy
- Uterine rupture if trial of labor after cesarean is performed

Treatment Recommendations

- Ultrasound confirmation of demise
- Induction is scheduled when the mother is psychologically prepared
- For mothers who refuse induction (rare), ongoing coagulation studies are warranted
- Recommendations for induction protocols are included in Table 9.1
- Notify staff of family's status
- Offer referrals for pastoral care, social worker, and grief counselor
- Discuss birth plan and requests for the labor and birth and care after delivery

TABLE 9.1 Interventions for Pharmacological Management of Fetal Demise

Past Delivery History	Recommended Approach for Birth
Nulliparous	Misoprostol (i.e., prostaglandin E1) vaginally or orally (400 mcg every 4–6h)
Previous vaginal birth	Intravenous Pitocin per protocol up to 30 mIU/min Pain management may include systemic morphine, Demerol, or Dilaudid IV/PCA or continuous epidural anesthesia
Previous cesarean birth	Foley bulb dilatation can be used as needed Intravenous oxytocin Pain management may include systemic morphine, Demerol, or Dilaudid IV/PCA or continuous epidural anesthesia

IV, intravenously; PCA, patient-controlled anesthesia.

  - Family members in attendance
  - Preferences for pain management
  - Placement of infant at time of birth (maternal chest, infant warmer, taken out of room)
- Prepare the family for alterations they may encounter when viewing the infant (misshaped head, bruising, malformations)
- Provide community-based resources (funeral home information, RESOLVE Support Group Information, grief groups)

Monitoring Recommendations

- Provide ongoing psychological support and referrals
- Uterine contraction monitoring is warranted to prevent uterine tachysystole
- Comprehensive postbirth physical exam and laboratory studies are warranted (Table 9.2)

TABLE 9.2 Maternal and Fetal Testing for Fetal Demise to Determine Etiological Factors

Fetal and Placenta Testing Recommendations	Maternal Testing Recommendations
Autopsy if no clear clinical etiology MRI if autopsy not conducted Radiographs as needed Fetal karyotype Indirect Coombs's test Placenta cultures (*Listeria*, parovirus B19, cytomegalovirus) Placenta studies	Hemoglobin A1c and fasting blood sugar Coagulation studies Toxicology studies Syphilis screening Thyroid studies (FT4, TSH) CBC Antibody screening as needed Kleihauer-Betke test TORCH panel Parvovirus serology Lupus anticoagulant Anticardiolipin anticoagulant Anti-B-2-glycoprotein 1 IgG or IgM antibodies Protein S & C activity

MULTIPLE GESTATION

The incidence of monozygotic twins is approximately 4 per 1,000 births. Monozygotic twinning occurs when a single ovum is fertilized and then splits. Approximately two thirds of twins are dizygotic, which occurs when two separate ovum are fertilized. Incident rates of dizygotic twin gestations are highest in African Americans (10 to 40 per 1,000). The incidence in Whites is 7 to 10 per 1,000 and Asian women have the lowest rates with 3 per 1,000 births (Fletcher, 2012). Naturally occurring triplets occur in 1 in 600,000 births and natural quadruplets occur in 1 in 700,000 births (Fletcher, 2012).

Adverse Effects on Pregnancy

- Maternal effects
  - Preeclampsia
  - Anemia
  - Preterm labor
  - Premature rupture of membranes
  - Hyperemesis gravidarum
  - Placenta previa
  - Hydramnios
  - Acute fatty liver of pregnancy
  - Venous thromboembolism
  - Fetal malpresentation
  - Abnormal placentation
- Fetal effects
  - Low birth weight
  - Intrauterine growth restriction
  - Respiratory distress syndrome
  - Intraventricular hemorrhage
  - Periventricular leukomalacia
  - Retinopathy of prematurity
  - Necrotizing enterocolitis
  - Patent ductus arteriosus
  - Neonatal nosocomial infection

  - Increased neonatal length of hospital stay
  - Cerebral palsy
  - Neonatal anemia
  - Neonatal polycytemia
  - Neurodevelopmental impairment
  - Twin-to-twin transfusion syndrome
  - Fetal death
- Delivery complications
  - Cesarean delivery
  - Placental abruption
  - Operative delivery
  - Malpresentation
  - Cord accidents
  - Postpartum endometriosis
  - Postpartum hemorrhage

Treatment Recommendations

- Monitor weight for appropriate weight gain patterns in pregnancy
- Assess for preeclampsia at each visit after 20 weeks
- Early or later gestational diabetes testing may be warranted in addition to screening at 24 to 28 weeks
- Educate on symptoms of preterm labor and preeclampsia
- Co-management with perinatologist is recommended
- Meet and greet with neonatologist upon admission
- Activity modification after 28 weeks
- Increase frequency of prenatal visits
- Plan the mode of birth based on fetal presentations, risk factors, physician preference, and maternal request
- Vaginal birth may be attempted for twin gestations where both fetuses are vertex
- A nonvertex presenting twin, monoamniotic twins, and triplets or higher order multiples warrant cesarean birth
- Consider delivery at 36 to 37 weeks for twins. Higher order multiples typically deliver prior to 36 weeks

Monitoring Recommendations

- Serial ultrasound to assess fetal growth
- Begin nonstress tests (NSTs) or biophysical profile (BPPs) weekly at 32 weeks as needed
- Assess for symptoms of preterm labor
- Fetal imaging studies if specific anomalies are suspected
- Neonatal complete blood count (CBC)
- Arterial blood gases and cord gases at birth
- Neonatal metabolic panel
- Neonatal bilirubin level

PLACENTA AND CORD INSERTION COMPLICATIONS

Placenta and cord insertion complications can lead to maternal and/or fetal morbidity and mortality. The risk associated with each condition varies and is based on multiple maternal and fetal factors. Table 9.3 includes the most commonly occurring placenta disorders and Table 9.4 includes the most commonly occurring umbilical cord disorders. Table 9.5 includes rare cord disorders but is included for reference purposes.

PREMATURE RUPTURE OF MEMBRANES

Premature rupture of membranes (PROM) occurs when the amniotic sac ruptures and labor has not occurred in a pregnancy more than 37 gestational weeks. The incidence of PROM is 10% (Jazayeri, 2013). Preterm premature rupture of membranes (PPROM) occurs when the pregnancy is less than 37 gestational weeks and ruptured membranes occur without labor. The incidence of PPROM is 3% (Jazayeri, 2013).

TABLE 9.3 Management of Placental Disorders

Disorder and Incidence	Risk Factors	Adverse Effects on Pregnancy	Types	Treatment and Monitoring Recommendations
Placenta previa 0.2%	Previous cesarean birth High, gravidity High parity Smoking Advanced maternal age Previous elective terminations Recent spontaneous abortion Male fetus	Nonreassuring fetal status Meconium-stained amniotic fluid Fetal anemia Maternal anemia Fetal death	(Quantifiable descriptions are preferred, although traditional terms are commonly used.) Complete: Os completely covered Partial: Os partially covered Marginal: Edge of the placenta is covered Low lying: Placenta in lower uterine segment but not covering os	Pelvic rest Delay birth until 37 weeks if possible Antepartum care with active bleeding: bed rest, monitor vital signs, bleeding with pad counts, uterine contractility assessment to rule out preterm labor, non-stress test every shift, continuous electronic fetal monitoring, CBC, Rh factor, intravenous fluids, two units blood available as needed, consider antenatal corticosteroids for fetal lung maturation If bleeding excessive, consider cesarean section

(*continued*)

TABLE 9.3 Management of Placental Disorders *(continued)*

Disorder and Incidence	Risk Factors	Adverse Effects on Pregnancy	Types	Treatment and Monitoring Recommendations
Placental abruption 0.5% to 1%	Advanced maternal age High parity Smoking Cocaine abuse Preeclampsia Trauma Rapid decompression of uterus with hydramnios or multiple gestation, preterm premature rupture of membranes (PPROM), past history of abruption, uterine malformations, fibroids, placenta defects, amniocentesis, shortened umbilical cord, subchorionic hematoma, thrombophilias, elevated alpha-fetoprotein, low socioeconomic status	Maternal and fetal anemia Fetal hypoxia Preterm labor/birth Antepartum maternal hemorrhage Couvelaire uterus Disseminated intravascular coagulation Hypofibrinogenemia Maternal shock Postpartum hemorrhage Renal failure secondary to shock Fetal death	Grade 1: Mild separation with slight vaginal bleeding with stable maternal vital signs and fetal heart rate Grade 2: Partial separation with moderate bleeding with uterine irritability, increased maternal pulse with stable blood pressure, nonreassuring fetal status may be present Grade 3: Complete separation with moderate to severe bleeding, maternal shock, abnormal vital signs, painful contractions, possible fetal death. Further classified as central, marginal, or complete	Monitor maternal vital signs, bleeding with pad counts, continuous fetal heart rate monitoring, intravenous fluid replacement, monitor coagulation factors, CBC, Rh factor, 3 units of blood on hand as needed If bleeding is controlled, vaginal birth may be possible; otherwise cesarean birth is warranted (Ladewig et al., 2014).

TABLE 9.4 Most Common Types of Umbilical Cord Abnormalities

Type of Disorder	Risk Factors	Adverse Effects on Pregnancy	Treatment and Monitoring Recommendations
Cord length variances Acordia: no cord present Short cord <35 cm Long cord >80 cm	None known	Short cords: Fetal movement disorders, intrauterine constraint, placental abruption, cord rupture, inability to deliver vaginally (<13 cm) Long cords: fetal entrapment, true knots, thrombi Straight cords: Adverse fetal outcomes	If placental abruption, oligohydramnios, or breech presentation occurs, measure and document cord length since abnormal cord length is a risk factor for fetal complications
Single umbilical artery Umbilical artery is absent Incidence 1% of singleton and 5% multiple births (Beall, 2012)	Twin gestation White race Gestational diabetes	Cardiovascular abnormalities, GI defects, esophageal atresia, renal defects, and multiple anomaly syndromes, chromosomal disorders (trisomy 18), intrauterine growth restriction, small placenta size	Detailed anatomy survey if two-vessel cord is discovered. Fetal echocardiogram, fetal karyotyping, serial ultrasounds for fetal growth in third trimester, neonatal ultrasound to examine for renal anomalies or other anomalies
Velamentous insertion (the umbilical cord inserts away from the placental edge, and the vessels pass to the placenta across the surface of the	Low maternal alpha-fetoprotein and elevated human chorionic gonadotropin levels	Low birth weight Preterm birth Ruptured vasa previa Nonreassuring fetal status in labor	Consider elective cesarean birth when fetal lung maturity established

(*continued*)

TABLE 9.4 Most Common Types of Umbilical Cord Abnormalities *(continued)*

Type of Disorder	Risk Factors	Adverse Effects on Pregnancy	Treatment and Monitoring Recommendations
membranes between the amnion and the chorion). Incidence is 15% in monochorionic twins and higher in triplet pregnancies (Beall, 2012)			
Vasa previa (fetal vessels are located in front of the presenting part of the fetus). Incidence is 1 per 2,000–3,000 births (Beall, 2012).	Low-lying placenta Placenta with accessory lobes Multiple gestation	Sinusoidal fetal heart pattern, fetal bradycardia, or fetal heart rate decelerations during labor may occur if rupture has occurred, nonreassuring fetal status, fetal death	Doppler flow studies for diagnosis and ongoing assessment Cesarean birth once fetal lung maturity established
True knots (1% incidence) (Beall, 2012)	Monochorionic twins Advanced maternal age Long umbilical cord length Multiparity	Nonreassuring fetal status	Cesarean section can be considered
Nuchal cord (20% of pregnancies have a single loop and 5% have multiple loops) (Beall, 2012)	Labor induction or augmentation, prolonged second stage, and fetal heart rate abnormalities	Nonreassuring fetal status Difficulty facilitating birth Fetal death (rare)	Continuous fetal heart rate monitoring in labor

TABLE 9.5 Rare Umbilical Cord Disorders That May Impact Pregnancy

Type of Disorder	Risk Factors	Adverse Effects on Pregnancy	Treatment and Monitoring Recommendations
Cord constricture (constriction or occlusion of the cord) found in 19% of stillbirth infants (Beall, 2012)	Family history is only risk factor	Majority of affected fetuses are stillborn	Unable to detect during the antepartum period
Cord hematoma (seepage of blood into the Wharton jelly surrounding the umbilical cord vessels)	Invasive prenatal testing procedures	Stillbirth is common in most fetuses	Doppler studies can diagnose the presence of the disorder If live fetus, deliver as soon as lungs are mature
Cord ulcerations Rare	Fetal upper intestinal atresias	Intrauterine hemorrhage	Unable to detect during the antepartum period
True or false cysts (located anywhere along the cord between the vessels). Incidence is 0.4% (Beall, 2012)	Fetal hydronephrosis, patent urachus, omphalocele, Meckel diverticulum, and chromosomal abnormailites		Diagnosis easiest via Doppler studies in first trimester Extensive review of fetal anatomy at 18–20 weeks to detect fetal defects Amniocentesis can identify a chromosomal abnormality Cesarean section once fetal lung maturity is established

(*continued*)

TABLE 9.5 Rare Umbilical Cord Disorders That May Impact Pregnancy *(continued)*

Type of Disorder	Risk Factors	Adverse Effects on Pregnancy	Treatment and Monitoring Recommendations
Cord varix (cystic dilatation that occurs in a portion of the umbilical vein) Very rare	None known	Fetal anomalies Nonreassuring fetal status in labor	Diagnosed with color Doppler flow studies Consider amniocentesis for chromosomal anomalies Nonstress test or biophysical profile at 32 weeks Serial ultrasound for fetal growth Scheduled cesarean birth recommended
Hemangiomas (hyperechogenic masses commonly at the placental end of the cord) Rare	Elevated alpha-fetoprotein levels Hydramnios Fetal hydrops		When cord tumor present, begin nonstress test or biophysical profile at 32 weeks Serial ultrasounds for fetal growth, detection of fetal hydrops, and vascular compression if tumor is present
Teratomas (germ cell tumors found along cord) Rare	None known		Ultrasound may identify an umbilical mass. If mass is present, monitoring is same as hemangiomas

Adverse Effects on Pregnancy

- Prolonged PROM (more than 24 hours) is associated with infection
- Chorioamnionitis
- Endometritis
- Placental abruption
- Nonreassuring fetal status
- Fetal restriction deformities (PPROM)
- Pulmonary hypoplasia (PPROM)
- Fetal/neonatal death (highest incidence if birth less than 32 weeks)

Treatment Recommendations

- Sterile speculum exam to determine PROM, estimate cervical dilatation, obtain cultures, and confirm a vertex presentation.
- Establish diagnosis with ferning test or AmniSure test.
- Expectant management should include avoiding vaginal examination and preventing infection via proper perineal hygiene.
- Induction can be considered via Pitocin administration or use of electric breast pump if desired in term gestations.
- If maternal fever, fetal tachycardia, nonreassuring fetal status, infection, advanced labor, or placenta abruption occurs, delivery is indicated.
- Ampicillin 2 g every 6 hours and erythromycin 250 mg every 6 hours is often administered to prevent infection.
- If group B *Streptococcus* (GBS) is unknown, treat for GBS until results are available.
- For PPROM that occurs between 26 and 34 weeks, administer corticosteroids for fetal lung maturation.
- For PPROM, some clinical trials have shown a reduction in cerebral palsy in infants who received magnesium sulfate therapy for 12 to 24 hours.
- If PPROM occurs, admission to a facility that can care for preterm neonates is required.

Monitoring Recommendations

- Second-trimester PROM is associated with increased fetal morbidity and mortality with management based on viability and gestational age.
- If PPROM, serial sonograms should be obtained to monitor growth and BPP for fetal well-being.
- PPROM without active labor warrants the administration of corticosteroids for fetal lung maturation and antibiotics to prevent infection.
- If in labor, intermittent monitoring after a NST is appropriate. If nonreassuring fetal status or a nonreactive NST, a BPP is indicated along with continuous EFM.

FAST FACTS in a NUTSHELL

Because premature rupture of membranes can have considerable risk, it is imperative that women be counseled that if leaking of amniotic fluid occurs, despite the amount, prompt medical evaluation is warranted.

PRETERM LABOR

Preterm labor (PTL) is the onset of labor that results in cervical change that occurs prior to 37 completed gestational weeks. The incidence of PTL is 12%. PTL accounts for 70% of neonatal morbidity and mortality (Ross, 2011).

Adverse Effects on Pregnancy

- Immediate consequences
  - Swallowing difficulties
  - Apnea
  - Respiratory distress syndrome
  - Necrotizing enterocolitis
  - Feeding intolerances

- Temperature instability
- Infections
- Patent ductus arteriosus
- Hypotension
- Preterm birth
- Bronchopulmonary dysplasia
- Neonatal death
- Nonreassuring fetal status
- Bradycardia
- Anemia of prematurity
- Intraventricular hemorrhage
- Long-term consequences
  - Cerebral palsy
  - Neurodevelopmental delays
  - Chronic lung disease
  - Hearing loss
  - Vision problems
  - Intellectual disability
  - Behavioral disorders
  - Social–emotional delays
  - Infant growth delays
  - Infant death during first year of life
  - Periventricular leukomalacia
  - White matter damage

FAST FACTS in a NUTSHELL

Near term or late preterm infants—those born between 34 and 36 weeks—have a higher incidence of complications including feeding difficulties, hypoglycemia, sepsis, respiratory distress syndrome, and jaundice, and warrant careful ongoing assessment in the early neonatal period.

Assessment for Risk Factors

- Decidual hemorrhage
- Uterine overdistension (multiple gestation or hydramnios)

- Cervical insufficiency
- Uterine distortion (history of DES exposure, fibroids)
- Cervical inflammation (bacterial vaginosis, trichomonas, chlamydia)
- Maternal inflammation/fever
- Urinary tract infection
- Hormonal changes (e.g., mediated by maternal or fetal stress)
- Uteroplacental insufficiency (preeclampsia, insulin-dependent diabetes, drug abuse, smoking, alcohol consumption)
- Personal history including past history of PTL
- Non-White race
- Extremes in maternal age (less than 17 years or more than 35 years old)
- Low socioeconomic status
- Low pre-pregnancy weight

Treatment Recommendations

- Obtain fetal fibronectin culture if PTL present
- If PTL present, screen for bacterial vaginosis, GBS, chlamydia, gonorrhea, and urinary tract infection, and treat if positive
- Test for anticardiolipin and lupus anticoagulant antibodies if PTL present
- If risk factors present, assess cervical length at 24 weeks
- If history of second-trimester losses or cervical insufficiency, consider cerclage placement at 12 to 14 weeks
- Administer 17-hydroxyprogesterone (Makena) intramuscularly 250 mg weekly; begin between 16-20 6/7 weeks and continue weekly until 37 weeks in women with risk factors
- Long-term use of tocolytics are typically not recommended but can be used to delay birth for 48 hours in order to administer corticosteroids for fetal lung maturity
- Pelvic rest during pregnancy is usually recommended
- Consultation with Maternal Fetal Medicine and Neonatology is recommended if preterm birth is likely

TABLE 9.6 Pharmacological Agents to Treat Preterm Labor

Medication	Recommended Dosage	Potential Side Effects	Contraindications
Magnesium sulfate	Loading dose 4–6 g IV over 20 minutes, then maintenance dose of 1–4 g/h depending on urine output and persistence of uterine contractions	Flushing, nausea, headache, drowsiness, blurred vision, respiratory depression, cardiac arrest	Drug toxicity warrants immediate discontinuation
Indomethacin	Initial dosage is 100 mg per rectum followed by 50 mg PO every 6 hours for 8 doses	Reduced fetal renal blood flow, oligohydramnios	Do not administer after 32 gestational weeks
Nifedipine	Initial dose 20 mg PO, then 20 mg orally after 30 minutes. If contractions persist, therapy can be continued with 20 mg orally every 3–8 hours for 48–72 hours with a maximum dose of 160 mg/d. After 72 hours, if maintenance is still required, long-acting nifedipine 30–60 mg daily can be used	Maternal tachycardia, palpitations, flushing, headaches, dizziness, nausea, alterations in liver function	Liver disease

IV, intravenously; PO, orally.

Monitoring Recommendations

- Assess for the presence of more than 6 contractions in 1 hour
- Advise woman of the signs of preterm labor and ask about PTL symptoms at each prenatal visit
- If treatment with tocolytic agents is required, monitor for side effects (Table 9.6).
- Initial treatment is bed rest but a gradual return of activity may be possible if contractions do not recur. If contractions persist, long-term bed rest or limited activity may be warranted

FAST FACTS in a NUTSHELL

In 2011, the Food and Drug Administration issued a Black Box Warning recommending that terbutaline should not be used in the treatment of preterm labor due to reported maternal death and adverse side effects.

10

Third-Trimester Complications

Various complications can arise in the third trimester that can impact the course of the rest of the pregnancy and create labor and delivery complications and possible adverse fetal effects. Prompt identification of abnormal conditions provides the health care team with essential data to plan and coordinate care for the pregnancy, labor, and birth.

After reading this chapter, the nurse will be able to:

1. Identify objective signs associated with an abnormal presentation
2. Discuss possible adverse fetal effects associated with intrauterine growth restriction and oligohydramnios
3. Define the appropriate monitoring recommendations for a post-term pregnancy
4. Compare and contrast preeclampsia and eclampsia
5. Identify screening techniques that should be performed when a size/date discrepancy is identified

EQUIPMENT

Ultrasound machine, electronic fetal monitor, Doppler, pregnancy wheel, blood pressure cuff, stethoscope, urine dipsticks, urine collection cup, reflex hammer, measuring tape.

ABNORMAL PRESENTATION

Abnormal presentations occur commonly during the second and early part of the third trimester in normal pregnancies. Abnormal presentation at term occurs rarely. Breech presentations occur in 3% to 4% of all pregnancies; transverse lies occur in 2.6% of all pregnancies at term.

Adverse Effects on Pregnancy

Breech Presentation

- Fetal injury (fractures, nerve damage, and soft tissue injuries)
- Fetal asphyxia
- Umbilical cord prolapse and obstruction
- Head entrapment

Transverse Lie

- Uterine rupture (if labor progresses)
- Prolapsed umbilical cord

Treatment Recommendations

- Breech presentations
  - External cephalic version
  - Elective cesarean
- External cephalic versions
  - After 36 completed weeks
  - Obtain informed consent
  - Review contraindications
  - External cephalic version using tocolytic agents is twice as successful

  - Use of epidural anesthesia doubles success rates
  - Nonstress test/biophysicial profile (NST/BPP) prior to procedure
  - Ongoing fetal heart rate monitoring
  - Ultrasound guidance to identify placenta location, fetal position, and fetal anomalies that would contraindicate a vaginal birth
  - Perform in a facility that can perform an emergency cesarean birth
- Vaginal breech birthing options should only be performed by experienced practitioners
- Ultrasound to rule out fetal or obstetrical contraindications to vaginal birth such as fibroid tumors, fetal anomalies, or placenta abnormalities
- Informed consent should be reviewed in depth by the physician if a vaginal breech birth is planned
- A double set-up in the operating room is often preferable in case emergency cesarean is warranted

Monitoring Recommendations

- If an abnormal presentation, obtain ultrasound prior to the onset of labor
- If an external cephalic version is scheduled, confirm persistent breech before procedure
- If breech vaginal birth is planned, review pelvimetry, estimated fetal weight, and other maternal and fetal factors

INTRAUTERINE GROWTH RESTRICTION

Intrauterine growth restriction occurs when the fetus does not achieve its genetically predetermined potential size due to impaired gas exchange and nutrient delivery in utero, which puts the fetus at risk for poor obstetrical outcomes. Etiological factors include: decreased oxygen-carrying capacity, dysfunctional oxygen delivery related to maternal vascular disease, placental damage resulting from maternal disease, abnormal fetal karyotype, presence of maternal infectious disease, and adverse environmental exposure history.

Adverse Effects on Fetus/Newborn

- Asymmetrical fetal growth abnormalities
- Necrotizing enterocolitis
- Neonatal thrombocytopenia
- Neonatal temperature instability
- Neonatal renal failure
- Respiratory distress syndrome
- Admission to the neonatal intensive care unit
- Intraventricular hemorrhage
- Intravascular hemorrhage
- Greater risk for metabolic syndrome later in life
- Oligohydramnios
- Abnormal Doppler studies
- Fetal or newborn death

Treatment Recommendations

- Serial ultrasound to monitor fetal growth
- Identify if symmetrical or asymmetrical intrauterine growth restriction (IUGR) is present
- Discontinue maternal smoking
- Nutritional counseling and supplements in underweight women with additional folate and magnesium
- Administration of maternal prenatal glucocorticoid administration for fetal lung maturation
- Amniocentesis after 34 weeks to determine lung maturity and plan birth
- Induction may be performed if Doppler studies are normal and fetal heart rate (FHR) is reassuring
- If nonreassuring FHR is present or abnormal Doppler flow studies are identified, consider cesarean birth

Monitoring Recommendations

- Fundal height measurements less than 3 cm warrant ultrasound assessment

- Abdominal circumference less than 2 standard deviations below head and femur measurements is diagnostic of asymmetrical IUGR
- Serial amniotic fluid volume assessments
- Umbilical artery Doppler flow studies
- NST or BPP weekly with amniotic fluid volume monitoring
- Continuous electronic fetal monitoring in labor is warranted

FAST FACTS in a NUTSHELL

Small-for-gestational age infants are those who are less than 10% of the birth weight of all fetuses of the same gestational age and are considered constitutionally small.

OLIGOHYDRAMNIOS

Oligohydramnios is a reduction in the amniotic fluid index of less than 5 cm or less than the fifth percentile (Baxter, 2012). It is also defined as an absence of a vertical pocket of amniotic fluid less than 2-3 centimeters. (Ladewig et al., 2014). Oligohydramnios can be associated with intrauterine growth restriction, blockage in the fetus's urinary tract, polycystic kidneys or any urinary obstructive lesion, Potter's syndrome, maternal use of prostaglandin synthase inhibitors or angiotensin converting enzyme inhibitors, or placental dysfunction/insufficiency. The most common cause is premature rupture of membranes (PROM) or amniotic fluid leakage. The severity of fetal effects is associated with the gestational age when it begins. The earlier it occurs, the higher the incidence of complications.

Adverse Effects on Pregnancy

- Fetal compression syndrome
- Pulmonary hypoplasia
- Meconium-stained amniotic fluid
- Fetal heart conduction abnormalities

- Umbilical cord compression
- Poor tolerance of labor
- Lower Apgar scores
- Fetal acidosis
- Obstructive uropathies
- Co-existing fetal abnormalities may include bowed legs, clubbed feet, a single umbilical artery, GI atresias, and a narrow chest secondary to external compression
- IUGR
- Small for gestational age
- Amniotic band syndrome
- Nonreassuring fetal status
- Cesarean birth
- Fetal death

Treatment Recommendations

- Rule out PROM
- Amniotic fluid lamellar body count, lecithin: sphingomyelin ratio, or phosphatidylglycerol concentration should be performed if early delivery is warranted
- Review symptoms of preeclampsia at each visit
- Systemic lupus erythematosus testing (can cause placental infarct or placental insufficiency)
- Maternal hydration (oral or intravenous)

Monitoring Recommendations

- Assess for preeclampsia and HELLP syndrome at each visit
- Antenatal fetal evaluation with weekly NST or BPP
- Serial ultrasound assessments once diagnosed
  - Amniotic fluid volume less than 5th percentile
  - Amniotic fluid volume less than 500 mL at 32 to 36 weeks

- Less than 8 cm indicates oligohydramnios in third trimester
- Less than 5 cm indicates severe oligohydramnios in third trimester
- Consider newborn evaluation for abnormalities in severely impacted infants
  - Chromosome testing as needed
  - Evaluate for congenital infection as needed
  - Ultrasonography of the genitourinary tract as needed
  - Appropriate radiologic evaluation of the gastrointestinal tract as needed
  - Electrocardiography and echocardiography as needed

FAST FACTS in a NUTSHELL

When examining a woman with IUGR, the fetus feels very close to the abdominal wall and it is extremely easy to identify the palpated fetal parts. In addition, the woman often either measures less than dates (smaller than expected) or has not had adequate uterine growth (as evidenced by measurement using measuring tape) since the last visit. These findings warrant considering a diagnosis of oligohydramnios and an ultrasound examination for amniotic fluid volume.

POSTTERM GESTATION

Postterm gestation refers to a pregnancy that has exceeded 42 weeks. The incidence is 3% to 12%, although higher statistics are likely associated with inaccurate dating (Caughey, 2011).

Adverse Effects on Pregnancy

- Maternal effects
  - Birth injury
  - Maternal death
  - Prolonged labor
  - Increased perineal injury

  - Increased operative vaginal births
  - Labor dystocia
  - Endometritis
  - Postpartum hemorrhage
  - Postpartum thromboembolic disease
- Fetal/newborn effects
  - Meconium and meconium aspiration syndrome
  - Neonatal academia
  - Low Apgar scores
  - Macrosomia
  - Stillbirth
  - Cephalopelvic disproportion
  - Shoulder dystocia with infant orthopedic or neurologic injury
  - Postmaturity syndrome
  - Nonreassuring fetal status in labor
  - Neonatal encephalopathy
  - Infant death in first year of life
  - Cerebral palsy
  - Birth injury

Treatment Recommendations

- Determine if the woman who goes beyond her estimated date of confinement is at risk for postterm pregnancy by assessing risk factors (primiparity, previous postterm pregnancy, male fetus, maternal obesity, and maternal family history of postterm pregnancy)
- Ensure accurate first-trimester dating. If unsure of last menstrual period or irregular menses, first-trimester ultrasound should be obtained
- Routine induction at 41 weeks with absolute delivery by 42 0/7 weeks
- Preventive interventions may include sweeping/stripping of the membranes, unprotected sexual intercourse, and acupuncture intervention
- If induction is scheduled, cervical ripening may be performed to reduce risk of cesarean birth

Monitoring Recommendations

- Antenatal testing twice weekly after 41 weeks to ensure fetal well-being (NST, BPP, modified BPP, or contraction stress test)
- Ultrasound to assess amniotic fluid volume; if oligohydramnios is present, induction is warranted
- NST upon admission; if nonreassuring fetal status, then continuous electronic fetal monitoring is warranted
- Monitor fetal descent carefully since cephalopelvic disproportion is more common in postterm pregnancies

FAST FACTS in a NUTSHELL

Women may ask how to stimulate labor in order to avoid prolonged pregnancy. Nipple stimulation (manually or by use of a breast pump), intercourse, or having the clinician manually strip the membranes can stimulate labor in some women.

PREECLAMPSIA/ECLAMPSIA

Preeclampsia is defined as a blood pressure more than 140/90 and proteinuria after 20 gestational weeks. Eclampsia occurs when preeclampsia is accompanied by seizures.

Adverse Effects on Pregnancy

- Uteroplacental insufficiency
- Low birth weight
- Placental abruption
- HELLP syndrome
- Disseminated intravascular coagulation
- Intrauterine growth restriction
- Oligohydramnios

- Nonreassuring fetal status
- Increased risk of future maternal cardiovascular disease
- Hepatic rupture (rare)
- Intracranial hemorrhage
- Temporary blindness (resolves in a few weeks; rare)
- Acute renal failure (rare)

Treatment Recommendations

- Increased prenatal visits as warranted
- Monitor labs weekly for mild preeclampsia, more frequently if disease progresses
- If severe preeclampsia or HELLP syndrome develops, delivery is indicated
- Severe preeclampsia warrants immediate hospitalization
- Seizure precautions with severe preeclampsia
- Referral to Maternal Fetal Medicine for collaborative care
- Magnesium sulfate treatment for severe preeclampsia to reduce blood pressure (BP)
- Hydralazine and labetalol for immediate BP reduction (typically given if diastolic is more than 105 mmHg).
- Intravenous magnesium sulfate if seizures occur
- Regional anesthesia is preferred pain management approach

Monitoring Recommendations

- NST or BPP weekly
- If accompanied by oligohydramnios or IUGR, twice weekly NST or BPP is warranted
- Serial ultrasounds for growth of the amniotic fluid volume (AFV) at least every 3 weeks
- Complete blood complete with platelet count, liver enzymes, renal functions, 24-hour urine collection for protein, uric acid, LDL
- Delivery may be performed as medically indicated

- If preterm birth is anticipated, betamethasone administration for fetal lung maturity is recommended
- Intensive nursing care is warranted for the woman on magnesium sulfate (Table 10.1)
- Continuous fetal monitoring in labor is warranted
- Vaginal birth is the preferred mode of birth for mild or moderate preeclampsia
- Severe preeclampsia or eclampsia warrants cesarean birth

FAST FACTS in a NUTSHELL

Subjective symptoms of preeclampsia include headaches, blurred vision, epigastric pain, right upper quadrant pain, sudden edema or significant weight gain, which warrant a prompt evaluation of the woman's blood pressure.

TABLE 10.1 Nursing Care for the Woman Receiving Magnesium Sulfate for Preeclampsia Management

Obtain baseline vital signs and oxygen saturation level, and then monitor every 15 minutes x 4, every 30 minutes x 2, then every 30–50 minutes.
Obtain baseline magnesium level; therapeutic range is 5–7 mg/dL
Assess breath sounds, presence of edema, and deep tendon reflexes every 1 hour
Quiet, darkened room environment in a side-lying position with limited visitors
Maintain continuous fetal monitoring throughout therapy
Insert Foley catheter and assess urine output every hour
Obtain labs and magnesium levels as ordered
Report adverse symptoms immediately: urine output less than 30–60 mL/hr, absent reflexes, abnormal vital signs or lab values outside normal range or preset parameters, shortness of breath, difficulty breathing, sudden chest pain, or marked sedation with difficulty arousing woman
Ensure calcium gluconate is available for emergency administration as needed (1 g given intravenously over 3 minutes)
Observe newborn for signs of magnesium toxicity after birth

SIZE AND DATE DISCREPANCIES

Uterine size that does not match expected gestational age is known as a size/dates discrepancy. Fundal height variations 2 cm above or below the expected fundal height after 24 gestational are considered a size or dates discrepancy.

Adverse Effects on Pregnancy

Increased Fundal Height

- Inaccurate dating
- Multiple gestation
- Hydramnios
- Fetal birth defects
- Gestational diabetes
- Large-for-gestational age fetus
- Macrosomia
- Infection (TORCH most common)

Less Than Expected Fundal Height

- Inaccurate dating
- Oligohydramnios
- Fetal birth defects (renal and urinary malfunction)
- Intrauterine growth restriction
- Placental insufficiency

Treatment Recommendations

- Establish estimated date of conception at initial visit by last menstrual period or ultrasound as needed
- Obtain early ultrasound in first trimester if unsure dates or irregular menses
- Obtain history of twins, infertility treatment, or previous macrosomia

- Review ultrasound at 18 to 20 weeks to rule out birth defects
- Once inaccuracy is identified, obtain ultrasound
- If oligohydramnios or hydramnios is diagnosed, perform further testing to identify etiology and follow management for those conditions

Monitoring Recommendations

- If large-for-gestational age or macrosomia is identified, consider repeat ultrasound at term for estimated fetal weight (EFW).
- EFW greater than 4,500 g warrants strong consideration for cesarean

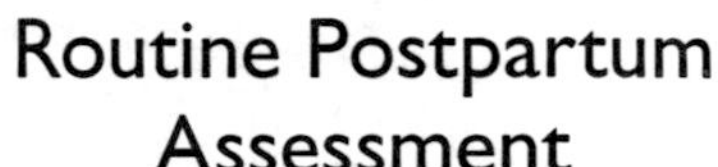

Routine Postpartum Assessment

For the new mother and her family, the postpartum period is most commonly a time of great joy, although many women are physically exhausted and begin a period of physical and psychological adjustment as the task of maternal–infant attachment and physical recovery begins. The nurse plays a key role in ensuring a smooth transition so the mother can adequately meet the physical and psychological tasks in the early postpartum period. The nurse serves as an expert facilitator of educational information and models appropriate child caring skills for the new family.

After reading this chapter, the nurse will be able to:

1. Describe risk factors associated with the fourth stage of labor
2. Identify normal parameters in a postpartum examination that are indicative of normal maternal physiological adaptations
3. Discuss normal psychological indicators that are present in successful maternal–infant attachment
4. State the components of a cultural assessment and its importance in providing holistic care for the childbearing family in the postpartum period

5. Evaluate the components of a comprehensive postpartum psychological examination that includes an assessment for postpartum mood disorders
6. Develop a comprehensive checklist for the prevention of psychological and physical complications in the postpartum period

EQUIPMENT

Blood pressure cuff, stethoscope, thermometer.

FOURTH-STAGE POSTPARTUM MANAGEMENT

The fourth stage of labor lasts from the expulsion of the placenta until 1 to 4 hours after birth (Davidson et al., 2013). The fourth stage is a time of rapid physiological change when a number of physiological complications can occur.

Frequency of assessments in the fourth stage:

- Every 15 minutes for the first hour
- Every 30 minutes times 2
- Every 4 hours for first 24 hours

Risk Factors for the Fourth Stage

- Postpartum hemorrhage
- Hematoma development
- Urinary retention
- Hypertension
- Hypotension
- Perineal edema
- Pain

Postpartum Physical Examination

The maternal postpartum exam includes a head-to-toe physical that assesses the woman's physiological responses to the completed birth process. The physical exam should include normal components of a head-to-toe physical including assessment of the heart and lungs, and an abdominal examination in addition to the components of the targeted postpartum exam (Table 11.1).

TABLE 11.1 Postpartum Maternal Physical Assessment

Body System	Normal Findings	Abnormal Findings
Breasts	Soft, no masses, beginning to fill. Nontender, pink in color with no redness or warmth, nipples protrude, no cracking or bleeding	Palpable masses, redness, tenderness, warm to touch. Nipples flat or inverted, cracking or bleeding. Pain with feedings or pain in breast area
Uterus	Firm, midline, round, located between the umbilicus and the symphysis pubis with a 1-cm reduction in uterine height per day after birth	Boggy, shifted to the side, nonmidline position, located above the umbilicus or size greater than expected for postpartum period
Bowel (abdomen)	Soft, nontender, positive bowel sounds, nondistended, positive flatus or positive bowel movement (BM)	Firm, notes pain or discomfort, no flatus or BM, decreased or absent bowel sounds, distension, palpable mass
Bladder	Able to void large amounts of clear yellow urine, which may contain lochia. Palpation reveals no palpable bladder via abdominal exam	Unable to void or voiding in small amounts, palpable bladder extends beyond the symphysis pubis upon abdominal exam. Cloudy urine
Lochia	Moderate rubra without clots or odor that decreases in the days postbirth and changes to lochia serosa and then lochia alba	Heavy lochia with clots or retained placenta fragments or trailing membranes present. Bleeding does not decrease and may increase, foul odor, presence of ongoing clots or clots large in size

(*continued*)

TABLE 11.1 Postpartum Maternal Physical Assessment *(continued)*

Body System	Normal Findings	Abnormal Findings
Episiotomy/ laceration	Perineum intact or sutures well approximated without excessive edema, bruising, or hematomas. No redness or odor present	Perineum with edema, not well approximated, sutures tense due to edema, foul odor, or hematoma
Hemorrhoids/ Homans' sign	No hemorrhoids present, no pain or tenderness present. No rectal abnormalities or fissures. Negative Homans' sign, no tenderness in calf area, pink in color with no redness or warmth noted	Hemorrhoids present, inflamed, tender, or fissures present. positive Homans' sign, redness, tenderness, localized area of warmth, or abnormal swelling
Edema (systemic)	Absent or mild non-pitting pedal edema	Excessive, worsening, pitting, facial or new onset edema

Psychosocial Assessment

A complete psychosocial assessment should be performed on each woman during the postpartum period (Table 11.2).

TABLE 11.2 Psychosocial Assessments in the Postpartum Period

Assessment Component	Normal Findings	Abnormal Findings
Maternal–infant attachment	Shows interest in caring for newborn, expresses concern for newborn, actively seeks out advice and guidance for care practices, looks at infant in an enface position, engages infant through touch and verbalization	Lack of interest in newborn; does not desire to participate in newborn care practices; does not look at, hold, or express desire to spend time with infant; unable to verbalize or anticipate infant care needs

(continued)

TABLE 11.2 Psychosocial Assessments in the Postpartum Period *(continued)*

Assessment Component	Normal Findings	Abnormal Findings
	Makes appropriate eye contact with newborn. Voices approval of infant including appearance or sex	Actions may be inconsistent, unable to interpret infant cues/needs. Reports dissatisfaction with appearance or sex of newborn
Depression assessment	Postpartum blues for several days often occurs but should not persist beyond several weeks. Typically occurs in 50% to 80% of women within the first 2 weeks of birth. No evidence of depression, crying, or feelings of worthlessness, sadness, or guilt beyond 2 weeks duration	Depression symptoms with feelings of worthlessness, guilt, sadness, crying, sleep disturbances related to emotional state that persist for more than 2 weeks and are not considered to be consistent with postpartum blues
Anxiety	Normal apprehension about infant care and breastfeeding is common. A concern for infant safety, infant well-being, and postpartum recovery is normal	Excessive anxiety that interferes with normal functioning. Panic symptoms, obsessive-compulsive symptoms, or symptoms of posttraumatic stress disorder can occur
Other	No abnormal psychiatric symptomology present	Women with a past history of psychiatric illness may be more at risk for adverse symptoms in the postpartum period

FAMILY ASSESSMENT

A family assessment provides essential information to ascertain if families are well prepared to care for the needs of the newborn in the postpartum period.

Components of a Family Assessment

- Family characteristics
  - Family members residing in the household including names, ages, and relationships between family members
  - Family structure, roles, and decision makers within the family
  - Health status of family members including intellectual, mental, and physical impairments
  - Familial trends of illness and health, longevity
  - Family support, encouragement
  - Expectations of children (ability to grow with children, future plans for children, influence of parents on children, relationship patterns)
  - Interactions among family members (loyalty, unity, and cooperation)
  - Family adjustment and functioning and ability to communicate
  - Family violence
- External relationships and influences
  - Neighborhood pride and loyalty
  - Internal and external relationships (balance of activity, creative play, planned groups support from outsiders, social relationships)
  - Involvement in community organizations (organization membership, knowledge of neighbors and community resources)
  - Ability to accept help from others and external resources
  - Spiritual or religious values and customs
  - Communication styles
  - Home environment (limitations, safety issues, etc.)
- Socioeconomic factors
  - Occupations of family members
  - Insurance coverage or enrollment in government assistance programs
  - Socioeconomic status
  - Use of community-based services

  - Education levels of family members
  - Ability to provide food and shelter
  - Immigration/legal status
- Health beliefs and practices
  - Mother's ability to perform self-care and infant care
  - Childbearing and infant feeding beliefs
  - Family dietary habits
  - Cultural values or customs
  - Self-help measures
  - Ability to understand health care-related teaching, advice, and newborn needs

CULTURAL ASSESSMENT

Family functions, customs, and norms are strongly influenced by their cultural background. A comprehensive cultural assessment should be performed to identify factors that may impact the postpartum family.

Components of a Cultural Assessment

- Communication: Primary language, ability to understand/read English, reading level, nonverbal communication patterns and norms
- Personal space: Perceptions of space, comfort level with proximity to others, eye contact, and comfort level with touching
- Social organization: Enculturation, acculturation, length of time since immigration, perceived head of family, role of elders, perceived leader in the family, and ethnicity. Other cultural factors may include geographical factors, age, religion, sexual orientation, and socioeconomic status
- Time: Concept of time, perception of time, past or present oriented. Some cultures may be persistently late, neglect time, or may neglect health care needs

- Environmental control: Locus of control, value orientation, visitors and views of visitors, previous use of alternative medicine in the past, any use of witchcraft, magic, prayer, or healers
- Health perceptions: Some cultures may neglect health needs or may not embrace preventive health care practices. Perception of good and bad health
- Spiritual/religious: Religious or spiritual beliefs, influences of religious organizations
- Occupation/education: Occupation and education in previous country and occupation in new country
- Biological variations: Ethnicity, skin color, body structure, nutritional preferences and deficiencies
- Food/nutritional preferences: Dietary habits, food preferences and dislikes

PREVENTIVE PRACTICES FOR THE POSTPARTUM PERIOD

FAST FACTS in a NUTSHELL

Postpartum depression can affect up to 20% of women, making it the most common postpartum complication. Identification of risk factors, early assessment, increased support, and prompt treatment can reduce the severity and negative consequences associated with postpartum mood and anxiety disorders.

Preventive Practices for Postpartum Depression

- Increase social support
- Attendance at new mother groups/support groups
- Education on newborn care and postpartum care
- Education on early signs of postpartum depression and postpartum psychosis
- Maintain a healthy diet with extra fluids

- Exercise regularly
- Maintain regular sleep patterns with additional naps throughout the day
- Utilize stress-reduction strategies
- If history of depression, monitor for any depression symptoms in the postpartum period
- For women with a history of severe depression in the past, consider antidepressant intervention in the postpartum period
- Women with antenatal depression should continue antidepressant therapy in the postpartum period
- Women with a history of a postpartum mood disorder should consider antidepressant medication in the postpartum period
- Women with bipolar disorder are at an increased risk of postpartum depression and postpartum psychosis and need close monitoring in the postpartum period
- Limit or avoid caffeine and alcohol in the postpartum period

Preventive Practices for Avoiding Postpartum Complications

- Prevention of postpartum hemorrhage
  - Frequent breastfeeding to reduce bleeding
  - Uterine massage
  - Monitor bleeding
  - Report bleeding of 2 or more pads per hour
  - Monitor and report large or ongoing presence of blood clots
- Prevention of bladder distension
  - Frequent voiding and emptying of the bladder
- Prevention of perineal discomfort, infection, and wound breakdown
  - Perineal hygiene with each void and bowel movement
  - Healthy diet with high fiber and increased liquids
  - Apply perineal medications for episiotomy, lacerations, or hemorrhoids

- Maintain ice to the perineum for first 24 hours
- Utilize sitz baths after first postpartum day
- For third- and fourth-degree lacerations, take a stool softener daily

- Prevention of alloimmunization
  - Administer RhoGAM within 72 hours of birth
- Treatment of anemia
  - Continue vitamin and iron supplements in postpartum period
  - If low iron levels occur as a result of postpartum blood loss, begin iron therapy immediately
- Best breastfeeding practices
  - Breastfeed every 2 to 3 hours
  - Ensure proper positioning with each breastfeeding session
  - Ensure infant is properly latched on during each feeding
- Monitor for complications
  - Assess for nipple tenderness, pain, bleeding, or cracks after each feeding
  - Report breast tenderness, redness, areas of concentrated warmth, or breast masses
  - Report fever, chills, foul-smelling discharge, or flu-like symptoms immediately
  - Report headaches, vision changes, epigastric pain, and swelling that begin in the postpartum period
  - Report any redness, areas of warmth, or tenderness in lower extremities immediately

12

Nursing Care of the Postpartum Woman

Nursing care and patient teaching for the postpartum woman and her family are a challenge since most women are discharged from the hospital setting within 48 to 96 hours of birth. Women giving birth in alternative care settings may be discharged as early as 4 to 6 hours after birth, whereas women who give birth at home may have ongoing care for only a few hours after giving birth. Routine assessments serve to identify potential postpartum complications and serve as a means to provide education to the woman about the normal physiological process that occurs after birth.

After reading this chapter, the nurse will be able to:

1. Describe routine nursing care in the immediate postpartum period
2. Discuss comfort measures that should be utilized in the postpartum period to reduce maternal discomfort and pain
3. Identify appropriate health promotion strategies that should be incorporated into the care of the postpartum family

4. Identify sources of support and education for new mothers and families in the postpartum period
5. Identify specific nutritional needs of the mother in the postpartum period
6. Name specific considerations for the woman who has given birth via cesarean delivery
7. Summarize breastfeeding recommendations, teaching, and support that should be provided to mothers after giving birth
8. Discuss the educational needs for mothers that have chosen to formula-feed their newborns

EQUIPMENT

Incentive spirometer, blood pressure cuff, thermometer, nursing pads, peribottle, sitz bath, sanitary pads

POSTPARTUM NURSING CARE IMMEDIATELY FOLLOWING BIRTH

- Perform complete assessment including vital signs every 15 minutes for the first hour
- Promote comfort by changing linens, obtaining a comfortable position, providing a new gown, and removing delivery room set-up materials
- Provide perineal care
  - Clean perineum with warmed soap or cleaning agent
  - For vaginal birth, provide ice pack to perineum
- Maintain hydration
  - Offer oral fluids and food
  - Maintain intravenous (IV) line with appropriate IV solution as ordered
- Assist with breastfeeding when infant is in the initial alert period while promoting family bonding
- Encourage early bladder emptying
  - Assess bladder status and bladder distension frequently
  - Encourage voiding as soon as mother feels the urge to void
  - If unable to void in the presence of a full bladder, catheterization may be needed

- Assess for complications and return to normal functioning
  - If epidural anesthesia used, assess for return of feeling and sensation in lower extremities
  - Assess for uterine atony, bleeding, perineal edema, hemorrhoids, hematoma formation, and complaints of pain
  - Assist mother out of bed for first time, assessing for lightheadedness, dizziness, feelings of fainting, or sudden bleeding
  - For cesarean birth, assess incision and dressing site for drainage and bleeding through the applied dressing
  - Assess pain level and administer pain medications as needed
- Ensure infant safety is maintained and mother is informed of infant status
  - Properly tag infant with identification band and put security alarm in place prior to leaving the room
  - If infant was removed from the room for medical indications, provide frequent updates on infant status to the mother
- Promote breastfeeding education and support
  - Assess nipples to determine if erect, flat, or inverted. Flat or inverted nipples warrant a referral to lactation services
- Begin teaching immediately as teaching opportunities arise, including breastfeeding information, perineal hygiene, uterine massage, and normal physiological changes in the postpartum period

POSTPARTUM COMFORT MEASURES

Afterbirth Pain (Uterine Cramping)

- Encourage mother to assume comfortable positioning, such as prone position
- Promote frequent ambulation
- Encourage mother to take pain medications 30 minutes prior to expected breastfeeding

Breast or Breastfeeding Discomfort

- General recommendations
  - Instruct mother to wear a supportive nursing bra
  - Position infant symmetrically facing toward the mother for optimal latch-on
  - Assess latch-on during breastfeeding to ensure as much of the nipple as possible is within the infant's mouth
  - Incorrectly positioned infants or those not properly latched should be immediately corrected to prevent breast or nipple soreness
  - Place a rolled washcloth or small towel under the breast to facilitate proper nipple position in women with large breasts
  - Report nipple cracking, bleeding, areas of pain, tenderness, redness, fever, chills, and flu-like symptoms immediately
- For engorgement
  - Frequent feedings
  - Massage breast prior to feeding to facilitate let-down
  - Avoid hot showers
  - Ice packs may be applied between feedings
  - Apply par-cooked cabbage leaves intermittently to decrease fullness
  - Pain medications as needed
- For non-nursing mothers
  - Wear tight-fitting bra during the day and when sleeping
  - Avoid any breast stimulation
  - Avoid hot water hitting breasts during showers
  - Pain medications as needed
  - Avoid any pumping or manual stimulation
  - Apply par-cooked cabbage leaves continuously to reduce milk supply

Constipation

- Limit narcotic pain medications in postpartum period
- Increase fluids

- High-fiber diet
- Early ambulation
- Daily exercise
- Stool softeners
- Women taking iron or calcium supplements are at risk for increased constipation

Hemorrhoid Pain

- Manually replace external hemorrhoids into rectum
- Cleanse with warm peribottle and wipe gently after each bowel movement
- Witch hazel pads
- Hemorrhoid creams
- Steroid foams or creams
- Side-lying positioning
- Increase fluids
- Raw fruits and vegetables
- High-fiber diet
- Avoid straining with bowel movements
- Stool softeners as needed
- Sitz baths

Perineal Discomfort or Pain

- Pericare with each void and bowel movement
- Ice application (20 minutes on followed by 10 minutes off) for first 24 hours
- Sitz baths (warm or cold per patient preference) after first 24 hours three times per day as needed
- Topical medications (witch hazel pads, hemorrhoid ointments, and topical steroid applications) as needed
- Report any signs of infection, breakdown of repair, redness, increasing tenderness, hematoma formation, foul-smelling discharge, fever, or chills

Postpartum Fatigue and Stress

- Encourage rest and sleep periods
- Limit visitors if mother overly fatigued
- Provide support and education
- Allow mother to discuss labor and birth
- Provide reassurance about her birthing experience
- Facilitate attachment and family visiting opportunities
- If traumatic experience, provide support, encouragement, and possible referrals for ongoing counseling or postpartum support
- Continue prenatal vitamins
- Healthy, well-balanced diet
- Ensure adequate fluids
- Encourage help at home with child care, household duties, and emotional support
- Referral to new mother support groups
- Encourage a gradual return to activity
- Evaluate every mother for signs and symptoms of postpartum depression

Postpartum Muscle Fatigue and Strain

- Proper positioning
- Pain medications as needed
- Gentle stretching
- Early ambulation

Postpartum Diaphoresis

- Frequent showering
- Change gown and bed linens frequently
- Increase fluids

POSTPARTUM MATERNAL NUTRITION

Calorie Recommendations

- Nonbreastfeeding, nonpregnant active woman with normal body mass index (BMI): 1,800 to 2,000 kcal/day
- Breastfeeding woman with normal BMI: 2,300 to 2,500 kcal/day

Nutrient Recommendations for Breastfeeding Mothers

Continuation of prenatal vitamin during breastfeeding is recommended. An increase in fluids is recommended. In addition, the following minerals are needed in higher amounts during lactation to ensure that adequate maternal stores are maintained and that breast milk contains essential minerals needed for infant growth and development.

Calcium

- Adult women: 1,000 mg/day
- Adolescent mothers: 1,300 mg/day
- Calcium carbonate is most readily absorbed and least expensive (Calcium Soft Chews, Caltrate, Os-Cal, Tums, Viactiv)
- Food sources: Milk, yogurt, buttermilk, part-skim mozzarella cheese, cheddar cheese, sardines, canned salmon, ocean perch, clams, collard greens, spinach, turnip greens, kale, beets, tofu, pancake mix with milk and eggs, molasses, English muffins
- Adequate vitamin D (400–800 IU) to aid in calcium absorption

Iron

- Pre-pregnant levels of 15 mg/day recommended
- Preexisting anemia or excessive blood loss at birth warrants supplementation (60–120 mg/day)
- Food sources: Oysters, beef liver, lean beef, tofu, and iron-fortified cereals. Other sources include potatoes with skin, watermelon, figs, spinach, chard, and dried fruits such as apricots, raisins, and prunes
- Foods that inhibit iron absorption include whole-grain cereals, unleavened whole-grain breads, legumes, tea, and coffee

Caffeine, Alcohol, and Fish Consumption in the Breastfeeding Mother

Caffeine

- Limit caffeine to moderate consumption during lactation (1 to 2 cups of coffee/day)
- Monitor infant for fussiness or jitteriness

Alcohol

- Limit alcohol to a small amount during breastfeeding. In general, one serving of alcohol takes approximately 1 to 2 hours to clear the breast milk, so a woman who drinks a single glass of wine may breastfeed after 2 hours. Subsequent drinks would take an additional 1 to 2 hours per drink and would warrant pumping and dumping to ensure the infant was not exposed to the additional higher alcohol levels
- Alcohol should not be consumed on a regular basis for breastfeeding women
- Mother may opt to pump milk prior to alcohol consumption and provide pumped milk
- If consuming alcohol, advise mother to breastfeed prior to consumption
- If larger amount ingested, encourage woman to pump and dump milk for several hours following alcohol ingestion

- Alcohol can reduce milk supply in the immediate hours following consumption by up to 23% (Lawrence & Lawrence, 2011)
- Do not sleep with infant in same bed if alcohol consumption has occurred
- Excessive alcohol consumption may interfere with mother's ability to care for infant

Fish Consumption

- Diets high in fish in general are considered healthier and provide excellent sources of omega-3 fatty acids, iron, zinc, vitamins A, B, and D, and protein.
- Although considered healthy, fish flesh may contain polychlorinated biphenyls (PCBs) and mercury, which can lead to neurological delays, learning disabilities, behavioral problems, and alterations in memory
- Limit farm-raised salmon, herring, and sardines to one to two times per month
- Limit bluefish, grouper, orange roughy, marlin, and fresh tuna to 6 ounces per week
- Limit cod, haddock, pollock, shrimp, tilapia, and chunk light tuna to 12 ounces per week
- Advise breastfeeding women to completely avoid swordfish, shark, king mackerel, and tilefish

INTENTIONAL WEIGHT LOSS AND DIETING COUNSELING

Women who formula feed should avoid dieting during the first 4 to 6 weeks postpartum to provide for recovery. Breastfeeding women need to maintain adequate caloric intake of 333 kcal/day the first 6 months and 400 kcal/day after 6 months to support milk production and should be counseled as follows:

- Encourage a healthy diet high in lean meats, fruits, and vegetables
- Do not diet during the first 4- to 6-week postpartum recovery period

- Rapid weight loss can reduce maternal milk supply in the breastfeeding mother
- Low-carbohydrate, high-protein diets should be avoided
- Increase fluids, especially water
- Avoid calorie consumption levels less than 1,800 kcal/day
- Encourage regular moderate exercise daily
- Inadequate calorie consumption is associated with postpartum fatigue, postpartum depression, and decreased bone mineral density
- Discourage fad diets and very low calorie diets or diets that advocate single-item intake
- Postpartum weight loss for women with a BMI greater than 25 is 4.5 pounds/month after the first month postpartum
- Set realistic weight loss goals of 1 pound per week
- Avoid high-calorie, non-nutritional food sources
- Avoid alcohol consumption
- Only small frequent meals only eating until satisfied

CESAREAN SECTION CARE

- Perform routine postpartum assessment immediately following delivery
- Monitor abdominal dressing for continued bleeding
- Mark any drainage with date and time
- Provide support of incision with ambulation and repositioning
- Assess Foley to ensure urine is draining properly and position draining to gravity
- Monitor urinary output and ensure greater than 30 cc/hr
- Early ambulation
- Leg exercises while in bed
- Compression stockings or intermittent pneumatic compression stockings during bed rest
- Pain medications as needed
- Assist with initial ambulation and care activities
- Assess emotional status, since some women may feel let down regarding mode of birth
- Encourage breastfeeding as soon as possible, provide assistance with initial feed

- Side-lying or football-hold positions for breastfeeding prevent pressure on incision site

BREASTFEEDING SUPPORT

- Encourage frequent feedings (every 2–4 hours)
- Provide tips to awaken a sleepy baby
- Ensure proper positioning and alignment
- Lactation consults for women with risk factors, abnormal nipples, and those experiencing feeding difficulties and as needed
- Observe initial breastfeeding
- Provide education on pumping, milk storage, and supplemental feedings with breast milk
- Encourage breastfeeding for first year of life
- Referrals to La Leche League, breastfeeding support groups, new mother groups, and community-based lactation consultants
- Discuss strategies for the working mother and continuation of nursing
- Look for the signs of dehydration and insufficient milk supply
- Observe infant in early postpartum period for adequate weight gain and wet diapers

FAST FACTS in a NUTSHELL

Breastfeeding is recommended as the preferred infant method for the first year of life. Inadequate nursing support and inability to successfully breastfeed prior to discharge from the hospital are leading risk factors for early breastfeeding discontinuation.

FORMULA FEEDING SUPPORT

- Reassure mother that decision not to breastfeed is her own decision
- Provide support to the mother who is unable to breastfeed based on medical contraindications

- Proper formula selection with iron in the first year of life (use of generics in general offers cost savings and is not contraindicated)
- Check expiration date on formula
- Educate on proper hand washing and equipment cleansing
- Proper mixing of formula
- Warm bottle under hot tap water; do not microwave or boil
- Do not over-dilute formula
- Proper storage of formula
- Only mix amount that will be used with a single feeding
- Do not reuse formula that has been consumed during a feeding, since bacteria growth can occur between feedings if more than 1 hour has passed
- Observe infant for constipation
- Encourage holding during feedings to facilitate attachment
- Do not prop bottles during feedings

FAST FACTS in a NUTSHELL

Women who choose not to breastfeed often report feeling guilty and may perceive disapproval from nursing staff. While it is appropriate to examine the woman's rationale for not breastfeeding and attempt to educate the woman and remove potential barriers, ensure you appear nonjudgmental and supportive of her infant feeding choice.

13

Postpartum Complications

Women who experience complications during pregnancy, labor, birth, and the postpartum period need additional assessment, intervention, and support during the postpartum period to prevent further complications. While some complications may appear prior to birth, others may not develop until the postpartum period. Postpartum complications can create additional stressors and concerns as the woman must now focus on additional treatment and care practices beyond the normal postpartum adaption while adjusting to her role and meeting the needs and challenges of caring for her newborn.

After reading this chapter, the nurse will be able to:

1. Identify the symptoms associated with breastfeeding difficulties in the postpartum period
2. Discuss symptoms related to postpartum infections and appropriate interventions for treatment
3. Define care practices that must be employed when caring for the woman with life-threatening postpartum complications
4. List the immediate interventions required for treatment of postpartum hemorrhage

5. Compare and contrast the different types of thromboembolic disease that can occur in the postpartum period
6. Define risk factors for postpartum urinary tract infections

EQUIPMENT

Breast pump, breast shields, breast pads, peribottle, urine dipsticks, urine collection cup, cultures.

BREASTFEEDING DIFFICULTIES, COMPLICATIONS, AND INFECTIONS

Breastfeeding is the recommended form of infant feeding for infants until the age of 1 year. The initiation rate of breastfeeding is rising, with 76.8% of new mothers in 2009 initiating breastfeeding as a primary feeding method; however, the rate of breastfeeding decreases dramatically with only a 25% continuation rate by the time the infant is 12 months of age (Centers for Disease Control and Prevention, 2013). Breastfeeding difficulties result in a substantial increase in discontinuation rates, so prompt intervention of problems can help in preventing early discontinuation in breastfeeding mothers.

Adverse Effects of Breastfeeding Complications and Infections

- Discomfort, pain
- Early discontinuation of breastfeeding
- Breastfeeding difficulties
- Maternal stress or distress
- Potential for feelings of failure

NIPPLE SORENESS

Normal nipple discomfort commonly occurs in most breastfeeding women as they adjust to the routine sensation of latching on. Nipple soreness is primarily associated with poor latch-on techniques, which can result in mechanical trauma. Nipple soreness can result in erythema, abrasions, fissures, bleeding, cracking, bruising, edema, and blistering.

Treatment Recommendations

- If the infant is improperly positioned, use a fish-hook technique to break the latch and reapply the infant until proper latch-on occurs. A fish-hook technique involves inserting a gloved finger into the neonate's cheek and pulling gently to break the suction seal with the nipple.
- Encourage the mother to change positions while feeding the infant so the position of compression varies with each feeding.
- Alternate positions with cradle hold, football hold, and side-lying positions.
- Proper care techniques include avoiding washing nipples with soap, air drying nipples after feedings, changing wet nursing pads immediately, applying drops of milk and massaging it into nipples after each feeding, and use of lanolin cream as needed.
- Breast shields can be worn between feedings if rubbing of the bra or clothing creates discomfort.
- Ongoing problems warrant a lactation consult with a breastfeeding specialist.

Monitoring Recommendations

- Observe the infant feeding session to ensure the infant is properly positioned in a symmetrical position with ear, shoulder, hip, and knee in proper alignment. The infant's tummy should be facing the mother's abdomen.
- Observe the latch-on position of the infant's mouth to ensure that the infant's entire mouth surrounds the areola and that the lips are flared. The tongue should be over the gum and cupping the nipple.
- Observe the nipple immediately after a feeding to ensure the nipple is symmetrically elongated with the

shape the same as it was at the beginning of the feeding. Nipples should show no signs of unilateral compression, bleeding, cracking, fissures, bruising, or abrasions.

FLAT OR INVERTED NIPPLES

Flat or inverted nipples can result in difficulty with proper latch on and can lead to infant frustration and crying as the infant is unable to properly latch on and feed.

Treatment Recommendations

- Position the infant far back on the areola so latch on is easier
- Teach the mother to use her thumb and index finger to pull the nipple out and create elongation
- Ice can be applied to help obtain an erect state
- A breast pump can be used to pull the nipple out from the breast

Monitoring Recommendations

- Have the woman demonstrate pulling the nipple out manually to ensure that the nipple is elongated and the infant can latch on correctly
- Women may use a nipple shield to encourage the nipple to protrude from the chest wall
- Ongoing difficulties warrant a consultation with a lactation consultant

BREAST ENGORGEMENT

Breast engorgement occurs when the milk comes in rapidly before the supply-and-demand mechanism is automatically regulated. Breast engorgement results in pain, hard, painful nodules, warmth, and the breast appearing taunt and overly distended in appearance. Women may have a fever up to 100°F during acute engorgement.

Treatment Recommendations

- Warm compresses or showers just prior to nursing to help with let-down reflex
- Circular systematic massage to assist with let-down reflex
- Application of ice packs or frozen bags of vegetables after feedings to decrease milk production
- Par-boiled cabbage leaves can be worn intermittently in bra to decrease milk production
- Anti-inflammatory medications (ibuprofen)

Monitoring Recommendations

- Observe for behaviors that can lead to engorgement, including delayed onset of nursing, infrequent feedings, early discontinuation of feedings, time limiting feedings, use of supplemental feedings, and changing the baby to the other breast too early
- Intermittent pumping can be used as a comfort measure but should be limited since over-pumping will result in stimulation of the milk supply and greater engorgement
- Ensure that frequent feedings are occurring

PLUGGED DUCTS

Plugged ducts occur when a milk duct or multiple ducts become obstructed. Typically redness, tenderness, heat, and a palpable lump may occur.

Treatment Recommendations

- Massage affected areas in a circular motion prior to feedings
- Apply heat or use a warm shower to assist with let-down
- Encourage frequent feedings
- Alternate positions to encourage adequate emptying

Monitoring Recommendations

- Ensure that frequent feedings are occurring
- Have the mother start each feeding with the affected breast
- Check that the mother is using a massage technique during feedings
- Monitor feedings, encouraging frequent feeding sessions
- Check that a proper bra with good support is available and being worn
- Untreated plugged ducts can lead to mastitis or a breast abscess

FAST FACTS in a NUTSHELL

Women with plugged ducts should aggressively treat the condition since it can further develop into mastitis. A warm shower with circular breast massage under the hot water can assist in unplugging ducts. The woman should immediately nurse the baby after finishing her shower.

MASTITIS

Mastitis is an inflammatory infection of the breast that occurs as a result of plugged ducts or milk stasis. Risk factors include maternal stress, cracked nipples, history of plugged ducts, and increased prolonged milk supply. Symptoms can occur abruptly and may include severe flu-like symptoms, fever, or red or hot area that is painful to touch.

Treatment Recommendations

- Immediate medical attention is warranted
- Warm moist heat to the breast is recommended
- Continue to breastfeed with frequent feedings
- Increase oral fluids, rest, and analgesics
- Antibiotics are required for treatment

Monitoring Recommendations

- Observe for ongoing symptoms
- Encourage woman to finish all antibiotics even if symptoms disappear

FAST FACTS in a NUTSHELL

Women with early postpartum breastfeeding complications and those who have not established successful breastfeeding prior to discharge are at greater risk for discontinuation of breastfeeding in the first 2 weeks following birth.

CESAREAN WOUND INFECTION/DEHISCENCE

Cesarean section wound infection occurs when the incision becomes infected via bacteria, which occurs in 3% to 6% of women who have a cesarean birth. Symptoms include fever, wound sensitivity, pus or drainage from the incision site, and lower abdominal pain. Dehiscence refers to the opening of the incision site and may occur with infection. Some infections may require the clinician to open the site to drain the infected area. Risk factors for infections include:

- Obesity
- Diabetes
- Emergency cesarean birth

- Chorioamnionitis during labor
- Prolonged labor
- Previous cesarean section
- Immunosuppressed state (HIV positive, AIDS, steroid administration)
- Staple closure at the time of surgery
- Excessive blood loss

Adverse Effects Postpartum

- Interference with breastfeeding
- Maternal fatigue
- Pain and discomfort
- Increased need for medical appointments
- Potential for ongoing illness and complications
- Risk of hospitalization
- Sepsis
- Perception of disfigurement
- Maternal distress
- Potential for maternal–infant attachment variations
- Potential for posttraumatic stress disorder (PTSD) or postpartum anxiety and mood disorders

Treatment Recommendations

- Culture incision site
- Antibiotics
- If wound is closed, clean area regularly with sterile saline or antiseptic solution
- Some wounds will need to be opened
- Open wounds require cleaning using sterile technique followed by packing with sterile gauze

Monitoring Recommendations

- Monitor vital signs, complete blood count (CBC)
- Inspect wound site regularly

- After patient teaching on wound care, observe the woman cleaning the incision/wound for proper technique
- Advise to complete antibiotic course

FAST FACTS in a NUTSHELL

Women with wound dehiscence should have frequent medical appointments to ensure that the wound is properly healing, that wound closure is beginning, and that infection is not developing or worsening.

DISSEMINATED INTRAVASCULAR COAGULATION

Disseminated intravascular coagulation (DIC) is a rare complication that occurs in 9 to 12.5 per 100,000 births and is most commonly associated with severe preeclampsia/eclampsia, placental abruption, amniotic fluid embolism, or hemorrhage. DIC is an abnormal clotting condition in which hemostasis becomes unbalanced and massive thrombosis occurs, which leads to depletion of platelets and coagulation factors.

Adverse Effects Postpartum

- Maternal anxiety and distress
- Separation from infant due to intensive care unit (ICU) hospitalization
- Interference with maternal–infant attachment
- Interference with breastfeeding
- Hemorrhage
- Shock
- Multisystem organ failure
- Maternal death

Treatment Recommendations

- If suspected, prothrombin time, fibrinogen, D-dimer, CBC, and a blood smear may be obtained for accurate diagnosis
- Transfer to the ICU is usually warranted
- Transfusions are needed to replace lost blood
- Intravenous fluids are given to increase blood volume
- Heparin is sometimes used to treat the cascade of hematological events

Monitoring Recommendations

- Observe for signs of abnormal bleeding such as bleeding from intravenous sites, gums, mouth, or nose. Petechia or bruising can occur and should be immediately reported.
- Since organ failure can occur, monitor urine output for signs of kidney failure. Dialysis may be needed in some cases.
- Monitor for hypothermia, hypocalcemia, and acidosis.
- Surgical intervention may occur, including hysterectomy or uterine artery embolization, so preparation for emergency surgery should be considered.
- Possible pharmacological interventions (ergot, misoprostol, Hemabate) warrant ongoing assessments and monitoring.

ENDOMETRITIS

Endometritis is an inflammation of the uterine lining that occurs as a result of a bacterial infection; it occurs in 1% to 3% of vaginal births and 5% to 15% of cesarean births. Symptoms typically occur 24 to 48 hours after birth and include foul smelling discharge, purulent discharge, uterine tenderness especially upon exam, fever, tachycardia, and chills.

Adverse Effects Postpartum

- Pain, discomfort
- Interference with maternal–infant attachment
- Breastfeeding difficulties
- Fatigue

FAST FACTS in a NUTSHELL

Extreme uterine tenderness disproportionate to the level of fundal pressure is often the initial sign of endometritis. Any women with increasing uterine tenderness should be fully assessed for other symptoms.

Treatment Recommendations

- Antibiotics
- Analgesics for pain and fever
- Diligent perineal hygiene

Monitoring Recommendations

- Monitor vital signs, CBC
- Assess fluid intake and encourage increased fluids
- If fever continues after 48 hours of antibiotics, additional workup for pelvic infection is warranted

EPISIOTOMY AND PERINEAL LACERATION INFECTION

Episiotomy infection is associated with purulent drainage, redness, ecchymosis, temperature elevation, warmth at the site of inflammation, or perineal abscess. Complications of perineal wound infection include dehiscence of the wound site, rectovaginal fissure, or hematoma formation.

Adverse Effects Postpartum

- Perceived disfigurement
- Maternal distress
- Pain, discomfort
- Need for future surgery

Treatment Recommendations

- Evaluate site and determine if wound breakdown has occurred
- First- or second-degree wound breakdown is treated conservatively with hygiene and sitz baths
- Third- or fourth-degree wound breakdown, purulent drainage, presence of an abscess, or systemic infection is treated with antibiotics
- Debridement and surgical intervention may be warranted for severe cases

Monitoring Recommendations

- Careful inspection is performed to identify the development or presence of necrotizing fasciitis
- Perineal debridement is often performed under local or general anesthesia
- Surgical closure is often performed immediately in an attempt to preserve the perineum
- Ongoing evaluation is warranted to ensure that purulent drainage, repeat wound breakdown, or other complications do not occur

HELLP SYNDROME

HELLP is an acronym that refers to a syndrome characterized by *H*emolysis, *E*levated *L*iver enzymes, and *L*ow *P*latelet count and is typically associated with severe preeclampsia, occurring in 0.5% to 0.9% of all pregnancies. HELLP syndrome is commonly characterized by an elevation in blood pressure, epigastric pain, malaise, visual changes, paresthesia, nausea and vomiting, seizures, and edema. In 20% of cases, DIC occurs as a comorbidity.

Adverse Effects Postpartum

- Separation from infant due to ICU status
- Alteration in maternal–infant attachment
- Interference with breastfeeding
- Anemia
- Jaundice
- Seizures
- DIC
- Hemorrhage
- Need for blood transfusions/blood products
- Maternal death

Treatment Recommendations

- When HELLP occurs in pregnancy, prompt delivery is indicated
- Intravenous fluids are needed
- Pharmacological interventions may include magnesium sulfate or antihypertensives (labetalol, hydralazine, nifedipine)
- Blood transfusions are sometimes needed to correct severe anemia

Monitoring Recommendations

- HELLP syndrome can be diagnosed using various criteria including the presence of thrombocytopenia (perinatal platelet nadir less than or equal to 150,000 cells/mcL), evidence of hepatic dysfunction (increased

aspartate aminotransferase level greater than or equal to 40 IU/L, increased alanine aminotransferase level greater than or equal to 40 IU/L, or both, with increased lactate dehydrogenase [LDH] level greater than or equal to 600 IU/L), and evidence of hemolysis (increased LDH level, progressive anemia).
- Ongoing laboratory studies are needed to monitor physiological changes including CBC, liver function tests, and urinalysis.
- Women often require admission to the ICU for close monitoring and ongoing treatment.

POSTPARTUM HEMORRHAGE

Postpartum hemorrhage is defined as more than 500 mL of blood loss from a vaginal birth or more than 1000 mL from a cesarean birth. Postpartum hemorrhage is typically related to uterine atony. Risk factors for uterine atony include:

- Overdistension of the uterus in pregnancy
- Prolonged labor
- Use of Pitocin in labor
- Epidural anesthesia
- Operative vaginal birth
- Third stage of labor more than 30 minutes
- Retained placenta
- Placenta previa

Adverse Effects Postpartum

- Interference with breastfeeding
- Maternal distress/anxiety
- Anemia
- Fatigue
- Need for blood transfusions/blood products
- Potential for PTSD
- Pain, discomfort related to pharmacological treatments

Treatment Recommendations

- Uterine massage is the immediate response for uterine atony and is performed until the uterus becomes firm
- Ensure the bladder is frequently emptied to prevent bladder distension, which can shift the uterus up and to the left and increase atony and bleeding
- Teach the woman how to self-perform uterine massage
- Encourage frequent, early breastfeeding
- Continue intravenous fluids with lactated Ringer's if the bleeding is heavy or uterine atony has occurred
- Consider an additional IV line with an 18-gauge catheter should blood products become needed
- Surgical intervention is rare but can include selective arterial embolization, SOS Bakri balloon tamponade, compression sutures, and hysterectomy

Monitoring Recommendations

- Women with risk factors warrant more frequent uterine assessments
- If atony or heavy bleeding exists, initiate a pad count and monitor for clots
- Uterine stimulants such as Pitocin, methergine, misoprostol, or prostaglandins may be needed, which warrant additional assessment
- If methergine is given, monitor blood pressure
- If bleeding persists, rule out other sources of bleeding such as genital lacerations, cervical lacerations, and blood coagulation disorders
- Notify clinician of uterine atony and ongoing heavy bleeding
- Monitor CBC for rapid falls in the hemoglobin and hematocrit, which can result in transfusion needs
- Monitor for complications of hypotension, severe anemia, and DIC

THROMBOEMBOLIC DISEASE

Because pregnancy and postpartum are hypercoagulative states, the risk of thromboembolic disease increases during the postpartum period. Additional risk factors include injury to the blood vessels and venous stasis, which often occur as a result of the labor and delivery process. Complications that may occur include superficial vein disease, deep vein thrombosis, and pulmonary embolism. Certain risk factors put the postpartum woman at risk for thromboembolic complications:

- Cesarean birth
- Prolonged immobility (long-term bed rest, mobility-related disabilities)
- Maternal obesity
- Previous personal or family history of thromboembolic disease
- Varicose veins
- Smoking
- Coagulation disorders
- Proteins S & C deficiency
- Polyhydramnios
- Preeclampsia
- Advanced maternal age
- Multiparity
- Anemia
- Incorrect positioning during labor and delivery
- Diabetes
- Malignancies

Adverse Effects Postpartum

- Pain, discomfort
- Interference with maternal–infant attachment
- Interference with breastfeeding
- Need for pharmacological interventions requiring in-patient treatment and prolonged monitoring

- ICU admission
- Respiratory distress
- Maternal death

SUPERFICIAL VEIN DISEASE

Superficial vein disease occurs when formation of a clot occurs in a vein, often at the site where an intravenous catheter was placed. Symptoms include:

- Warmth at the site
- Tenderness
- Redness
- Tender, palatable soft nodule may be present
- Normal temperature or low-grade fever
- Possible increase in pulse rate

Treatment Recommendations

- Moist heat
- Elevation of affected extremity
- Compression stocking
- Analgesics
- Bed rest

Monitoring Recommendations

- Assess site regularity for increase in redness, red streaking on the extremity, fever, tachycardia
- Monitor vital signs
- Assess for complications related to pulmonary embolism (chest pain, respiratory difficulties)
- If deep vein thrombosis (DVT) is suspected, additional screening is warranted

DEEP VEIN THROMBOSIS

DVT occurs when there is a formation of a blood clot (thrombus) in a deep vein, typically in the lower extremities with the left leg being affected more often. Symptoms include:

- Palpable nodule
- Edema
- Initially a low-grade fever then a high fever commonly occur
- Variations in limb circumferences more than 2 cm
- Pale limb color with limb cool to touch
- Referred pain to popliteal area, inguinal area, lateral tibial area, lower leg, and foot

FAST FACTS in a NUTSHELL

While a positive Homans' sign is a specific finding, it has a low detection rate and is no longer recommended as a standard screening tool for a normal postpartum exam.

Treatment Recommendations

- Anticoagulants
- Thrombin inhibitors are sometimes used if heparin is contraindicated
- Vena cava filters may be indicated for some patients but use in postpartum is rare
- Compression stockings

Monitoring Recommendations

- Monitor site for temperature and color
- Monitor vital signs
- Assess for bleeding and bruising

- Monitor international normalized ratio/prothrombin time (INR/PT) levels if the patient is on anticoagulants
- Assess extremities, removing compression stockings periodically

PULMONARY EMBOLISM

Pulmonary embolism is a complication that occurs when a DVT breaks free and travels to the lung artery. Symptoms include:

- Shortness of breath
- Anxiety, feeling of dread
- Coughing, including coughing up blood
- Difficulty breathing
- Arrhythmia, tachycardia

Treatment Recommendations

- Medical emergency that warrants immediate hospitalization
- Intravenous fluids
- Thrombolytics if no contraindications and if the woman meets the criteria for immediate treatment to dissolve the clot
- Anticoagulants
- Vena cava filters are rarely used in the postpartum population
- Compression stockings

Monitoring Recommendations

- Monitor vital signs
- Assess for bleeding and bruising
- Monitor INR/PT levels if the patient is on anticoagulants

URINARY TRACT INFECTIONS (UTIs)

Risks of UTIs in the postpartum period include bladder trauma, introduction of bacteria into the bladder during labor and birth, bacterial shedding, and frequent cauterizations during labor and delivery.

Adverse Effects Postpartum

- Pain, discomfort
- Urinary frequency, urgency, hesitancy, dysuria
- Risk for pyelonephritis
- Sepsis

Treatment Recommendations

- Antibiotics
- Increase oral fluids
- Proper perineal hygiene
- Acidic fluids such as cranberry juice
- Vitamin C supplements

Monitoring Recommendations

- Assess for frequent bladder emptying habits every 2 to 4 hours
- Monitor vital signs, urinalysis, urine culture results, and CBC
- Assess for symptoms of UTI including dysuria, frequency, urgency, hesitancy, dribbling, nocturia, and suprapubic pain
- Assess for worsening symptoms such as high fever, flu-like symptoms, flank pain, nausea, and vomiting, which could indicate progression to pyelonephritis

14

Postpartum Complications With Psychosocial Implications

While all postpartum complications can result in psychosocial implications, some have more psychosocial impact than physical alterations. Postpartum mood and anxiety disorders (PMAD) that occur after birth can have a significant impact on the mother, her family, and maternal–infant attachment. Women with a previous mental health condition are at greater risk to develop a PMAD and need close monitoring and additional support during the postpartum period. Pregnancy loss is a catastrophic event that has considerable psychological implications. Women with infants who require prolonged hospitalization often experience stress and anxiety when they are discharged without their infants.

Some women may experience a traumatic birth that results in poor outcomes leaving the woman with disappointment, sadness, and unanswered questions related to the birth experience. These women require additional support, education, and opportunities for verbalization about the outcomes related to the birthing process.

After reading this chapter, the nurse will be able to:

1. Compare and contrast the different types of postpartum mood and anxiety disorders (PMADs)
2. Define nursing interventions that are appropriate for the woman who has experienced a pregnancy loss
3. List strategies to foster maternal–infant attachment in infants who experience a prolonged hospitalization
4. Discuss psychological implications associated with traumatic birth

EQUIPMENT

Memory box.

POSTPARTUM MOOD AND ANXIETY DISORDERS (PMADs) AND MENTAL ILLNESS

PMADs and mental illness are the most commonly occurring complications related to childbearing. A woman is more likely to be hospitalized for a psychiatric indication in the first year following childbirth than at any other time of her life (Davidson, 2012). Prompt identification and treatment are crucial to prevent maternal and familial adverse outcomes (Table 14.1). Women with underlying mental illnesses are more at risk for the development of symptoms in the postpartum period and warrant additional assessment and monitoring during the postpartum period.

Adverse Effects Postpartum

- Alterations in maternal–infant attachment and family interactions
- Potential for interference with breastfeeding
- Social isolation
- Suicide

TABLE 14.1 Postpartum Mood and Anxiety Disorders, Symptoms, and Treatment

Type of Illness	Incidence	Symptoms	Treatment
Postpartum depression	Up to 25% of all births	Sadness, insomnia, disinterest in activities, guilt, hopelessness, labile moods, crying, fatigue, exhaustion, excessive worrying, difficulty concentrating, lack of sexual desire	All women should be screened in the postpartum period using an established instrument, behavioral therapies, support groups, new mother groups. Selective serotonin reuptake inhibitors (SSRIs) are the pharmacological treatment of choice since they are safe for breastfeeding
Postpartum anxiety disorder	Can occur in up to 20% of all postpartum women	Nervousness, hypervigilance with baby, lability, appetite changes, sleep disruption, distractibility, memory loss	Screening with an anxiety instrument is recommended. SSRIs are often used when medication is warranted. Cognitive behavioral therapy has proven to be helpful
Posttraumatic stress disorder (PTSD)	Can occur in 1.5% to 5.6% of women	Intrusive symptoms: flashbacks, nightmares Avoidance symptoms: difficulty with maternal–infant attachment, avoidance of sex, pregnancy, and birth-related issues Arousal symptoms: irritability, sweating, trembling, sleep disturbances	Screening is based on history. PTSD instruments can be used. Behavioral therapies and support groups are often used. Medication intervention may include SSRIs. Screening for other psychological comorbidities is recommended
Postpartum psychosis	Occurs in 0.1%–0.2% of all pregnancies	Cognitive impairment, bizarre behaviors, lack of insight, thought disorganization, delusions of reference or persecution, homicidal or suicidal ideations, hallucinations, delirium-like appearance, intense mood swings, acting out of control, and command hallucinations	Prompt emergency inpatient psychiatric hospitalization is warranted. Antipsychotics, mood stabilizers, and benzodiazepines are often used. If bipolar disorder has been ruled out, antidepressants may be prescribed. Supportive behavioral therapeutic therapies can be used in addition to aggressive pharmacological interventions

FAST FACTS in a NUTSHELL

Since postpartum mood and anxiety disorders are the most commonly occurring complications of childbirth, universal screening for all of the postpartum period should occur prior to discharge and at the postpartum visit. Women with risk factors need more frequent assessments during the first 6 weeks postpartum.

PREGNANCY LOSS

Women who experience a pregnancy loss after 20 weeks typically give birth in a hospital setting and usually receive ongoing care in the postpartum unit. The woman who suffers a loss requires the same physiological care as other postpartum women with special attention to her psychological and social needs during this difficult time.

Adverse Effects on Pregnancy and Postpartum

- Grief, sadness, anxiety, hopelessness
- Postpartum mood or anxiety disorders
- Risk of posttraumatic stress disorder (PTSD)
- Extreme anxiety in future pregnancies

Treatment Recommendations

- Offer placement on an alternative unit if the woman desires
- Assist the woman with beginning the grief process
- Provide an opportunity for the woman and her family to hold the infant
- Provide an empathetic caring approach
- Answer questions honestly knowing the woman often repeats the same questions
- Take cues from the woman on her comfort level and desire to have the infant remain at the bedside

- Customize postpartum teaching to meet her needs
- Encourage a firm-fitting bra as soon as possible to reduce engorgement
- Offer appropriate consultations as the woman/family requests: grief counselor, clergy
- Prepare a memory box and physical mementos for the woman to take home

Monitoring Recommendations

- Provide monitoring of visitors based on woman's requests and desires
- Provide support for family members and siblings
- While the infant is in the room, offer to either stay with the woman or ask her if she would prefer to be alone
- Refer to support groups, community resources, and specialty groups that deal with infant loss, such as Resolve through Sharing
- If an autopsy is desired, ensure paperwork and fetus are properly processed once the family has said their final goodbye
- Perform appropriate postmortem care
- If woman is stable and desires an early discharge, obtain an order for early release
- Arrange for follow-up care in 2 weeks
- Discuss risks of postpartum depression and bereavement issues
- Call the woman after discharge to check on her and offer condolences for her loss

FAST FACTS in a NUTSHELL

Most facilities have a standardized memory box or protocol that provides a detailed checklist of what to include in the discharge kit for the family. Mementos may include photos, infant identification band, blanket, cap, fingerprints, foot and hand molds, crib card, lock of hair, and clothing worn by the infant.

PROLONGED INFANT HOSPITALIZATION

Prolonged infant hospitalizations may occur as a result of prematurity, congenital abnormalities, or adverse health conditions that have occurred in the early newborn period. Mothers and families who are discharged without their infants face a great deal of anxiety, stress, and sadness.

Adverse Effects Postpartum

- Maternal stress/distress
- Interference with breastfeeding
- Alterations with breast pumping
- Potential for maternal–infant attachment issues
- Separation from infant
- Maternal fatigue from frequent visits to hospital
- Anxiety, sadness related to discharge without infant

Treatment Recommendations

- Send the mother home with photos and mementos of the baby
- Encourage the mother to call and check on her baby whenever she wants and provide phone contact numbers
- Encourage visitation whenever possible
- Encourage breastfeeding and provide instructions for pumping and proper milk storage

Monitoring Recommendations

- Assess the mother for postpartum depression and reaction related to ongoing need for hospitalization of her baby
- Maternal fatigue is common so monitor to ensure proper rest and maternal nutritional needs are met

- Assist the mother with learning specific care needs of her infant and allow her to provide as much care as she is comfortable with during the hospitalization
- When possible, have the mother stay overnight prior to discharge to ensure that all questions and needs of the infant are met prior to discharge
- Monitor nursery feedings and provide assistance with feedings as needed
- Ensure parents know how to properly use a car seat prior to discharge
- Refer to community resources, support groups, new mother groups, and counseling as needed

FAST FACTS in a NUTSHELL

Separation from a newborn due to a prolonged hospitalization can create considerable stress for the family. Providing updates to the parents upon their arrival to the hospital facility and including them in all components of care can help promote family attachment.

TRAUMATIC BIRTH AND POOR OUTCOMES

Women who experience traumatic births or poor maternal or newborn outcomes may experience physical and psychosocial consequences. Some outcomes may be unexpected, such as an unknown newborn defect, where others may be known prior to birth.

Adverse Effects Postpartum

- PTSD
- Anxiety

- Postpartum depression
- Adjustment disorders
- Fear with future pregnancies
- Maternal distress/stress
- Ongoing physical side effects or complications

Treatment Recommendations

- Allow the mother to voice her feelings and reactions to the events
- Encourage her to express distrust, anger, or other negative feelings that she may feel are related to the events and outcome
- Validate her feelings and reassure her that what she is feeling is appropriate
- Refer the mother for counseling if signs of distress or altered coping are present
- Referrals to support groups for infant loss, postpartum groups, and appropriate specialty groups
- Women who experience a traumatic birth are more at risk for postpartum mood disorders
- Many women will experience significant anxiety and distress in subsequent pregnancies, making effective strategies important for both current and future birth-related events

Monitoring Recommendations

- Perform screening for postpartum depression
- Assess for adjustment disorders or symptoms that indicate an inability to cope with outcomes
- Psychological and social support requires frequent monitoring to determine if symptoms are improving, stabilizing, or worsening
- If postpatum depression is present, monitor for suicidal ideations

- Assess stage of grieving and determine if mother is appropriately moving through each stage or if support services are needed

FAST FACTS in a NUTSHELL

If a woman experiences a birth injury or gives birth to an infant with a known congenital defect, refer her to a specialty group that focuses on supporting new parents. Many online support groups are available for rare and uncommon disorders, providing a platform for members to share and gather information.

Appendices

Antepartum Skills

Some basic antepartum skills are imperative to basic obstetrical practice. All procedures should be approached in a systematic manner using a calm, caring approach that conveys respect.

GENERALIZED APPROACH TO ASSESSMENT AND PROCEDURES

Background

Prior to performing any assessment or procedure, certain professional procedures are imperative. Establishing a therapeutic relationship can establish trust, decrease anxiety, and enhance communication.

Procedure and Rationale

1. Prior to meeting the patient and family, determine any pertinent information that would impact the relationship from other care providers and the patient's chart.

Certain factors may impact the initial interaction so obtaining specific information can enhance the initial meeting.

2. Introduce yourself by name and ask the patient how she and family members prefer to be addressed. Certain cultural groups may feel more comfortable being called Mrs. or Ms. or Mr. instead of their first names. Respect for cultural and personal preferences conveys respect and preserves dignity.
3. Explain all information in a manner that the patient can understand. Families for which English is a second language should be offered an intepreter for all interactions. Women with certain disabilities, such as those who are deaf, may need additional provisions as well.
4. Always provide privacy, appropriate draping, or coverage, and ask the woman if she prefers to have the assessment or procedure performed without family present.
5. Always ask the woman her name and check the identification band to ensure it is the correct patient.
6. Always wash your hands using proper handwashing technique prior to any patient contact.
7. Always explain the procedure prior to starting any task and ask permission prior to touching the woman.
8. Provide emotional reassurance during the assessment or procedure to decrease anxiety, increase patient understanding, and provide integrated patient teaching.
9. Upon completion of the task, briefly explain your findings or give reassurance that things went well. Answer any questions and address any concerns the patient may have.
10. Wash your hands after each patient encounter to prevent transmission of infection.
11. Document appropriate findings and convey data to other health care team members as needed.

ASSISTING WITH A PELVIC EXAM

Background

A pelvic exam is performed at the initial obstetrical visit and then as needed during pregnancy. The initial pelvic exam serves to assess for pregnancy-related physiological changes, identify abnormalities or variances in the reproductive structures, estimate the gestational age of the pregnancy, and collect cultures and a Pap smear.

Equipment

Speculum, gloves, Pap smear preserving liquid solution or glass slide, collection instruments (brush, spatula/broom), large swabs, culture collection tubes, lubricant, and spray fix (if glass slide is used). Equipment should be set up on a clean tray or area in close proximity to the examination table.

Procedure and Rationale

1. Provide privacy for the patient to change and provide the patient with a drape or sheet. Providing privacy conveys respect and preserves dignity and decreases modesty.
2. Assist the patient as needed to sit on the exam table and evaluate for risk factors that can impact exam process. Women with a past history of abuse or posttraumatic stress disorder may need additional preparation, support, and time for procedure.
3. Ask patient to slide down to the end of the examination table so that the hips are just over the edge of the exam table with the hips tilted slightly upward. Tilting the pelvis slightly positions the cervix so it is easier to visualize. Provide assistance so the woman is comfortable, with the head of the table slightly elevated to prevent

hypotension. Ensure that patient safety is maintained. Women with physical disabilities may need additional staff present to maintain safety.

4. Warm the speculum under warm water and hand to the clinician performing pelvic exam. While lubricant cannot be used if obtaining specimens, warmed water can provide some lubrication to ease discomfort.
5. Encourage the woman to breathe gently during the exam and not to contract pelvic muscles. You can also instruct the woman to bear down at the time of speculum insertion. Continue to provide emotional reassurance and explanation of what is occurring throughout the exam. Verbalizing information, encouraging muscle relaxation, and providing a distraction can ease the anxiety and decrease discomfort during the exam.
6. Hand the clinician the Pap smear collection instruments. Ensure that each specimen is properly labeled with the correct patient identification label. It is imperative that specimens contain all pertinent patient identification.
7. Hand the clinician the culture collection tools and verify they are properly labeled to ensure proper patient identification.
8. At the completion of the speculum exam, take the speculum and any instruments from the clinician and put aside. Contaminated instruments should be stored in a contained location so proper cleaning is ensured. Assist with lubricant for clinician as needed.
9. Provide reassurance and explanation as the pelvic exam is completed with a bimanual exam. These measures decrease anxiety and give the woman a sense of control. Some clinicians may perform a rectal exam. The woman should be informed during a pause in the exam process before beginning the rectal exam.
10. Upon completion of the exam, assist the woman into a sitting position by placing your hands on her knees and instructing her to scotch up on the table. Then offer the woman a hand to rise to a seated position. Ensure that the woman is not lightheaded upon sitting up. Hypotension can occur in pregnant women as a result of increased pressure on the vena cava.

11. Provide the woman with a tissue to wipe and remove lubricant x that was inserted during the exam from the vagina.
12. Ensure all specimens are properly labeled, document that they have been processed and sent to the lab for processing, and place in the proper location for transport to the lab.

OBTAINING FETAL HEART BEAT/RATE IN THE FIRST TRIMESTER

1. Have the woman empty her bladder since a full bladder sometimes interferes with assessing the true position and size of the uterus.
2. Obtain pertinent menstrual history including last menstrual period (LMP), regularity of menses, normalcy of LMP, previous menstrual period, menstrual data including onset of menarche, cycle length and duration, and normal bleeding patterns. Determine if any birth control method x, use of fertility agents, or other medication were in use at the time of conception that could impact menses. Assess if there is any history of multiple births, fibroids, ovarian cysts, or pelvic structure abnormalities. Certain factors can impact the timing of conception so assessment of possible etiological factors is imperative.
3. Calculate estimated date of conception to determine estimated gestational age prior to examination. While a fetal heart rate (FHR) is present on ultrasound at 6 gestational weeks, the ability to auscultate the FHR via abdominal exam typically does not occur until 10 to 12 weeks. In women with certain factors, it may be difficult to obtain a FHR. Common factors include obesity, retroverted uterus, incorrect dating, placement of gestational sac within the uterus, or presence of anterior fibroids.
4. Lower the woman's head to the lowest comfortable position. Palpate uterus via gently palpating above the symphysis pubis. A 12-week gestational size should be

palpable just above the symphysis pubis. If the uterus is less than 10- to 12-week size, it is likely that the FHR may not be detectable via an abdominal auscultation method. Lowering the head often aids in having the uterus "pop up" and move into the best anatomical position.

5. If the uterus is palpable, attempt to locate the FHR using a ultrasound Doppler device. An ultrasound transmission gel should be applied to the device. Begin by gently applying pressure and moving the device slowly over the uterus to auscultate the FHR. The FHR does not transmit through bone, so keep the device location above the symphysis pubis. Adjusting the angle of the device may aid in detecting the FHR. Move the device in a slow, steady, systematic manner to cover all areas of the uterus that are above the symphysis pubis.
6. Once the fetal heart beat is obtained, count the beats for 30 to 60 seconds to determine the FHR. The FHR should be between 110 and 160 bpm. If the FHR is less than 110 bpm, obtain the maternal pulse to ensure that the heart rate is the fetus's and not the maternal rate.
7. If the FHR is not detected, the woman can be offered an ultrasound examination to confirm dates and viability. If no other risk factors are present, and the woman denies bleeding and pain, the woman can be given the option of returning in 1 week for reassessment. At that time, if the FHR is still not detected, an ultrasound examination is warranted.

ASSISTING WITH AMNIOCENTESIS

Background

An amniocentesis is most commonly performed during the second trimester to obtain an amniotic fluid specimen to perform a chromosomal analysis to identify possible genetic anomalies in the fetus. Amniocentesis can also be performed as a means to reduce amniotic fluid or to determine fetal lung maturity status if a preterm birth is warranted.

Equipment

Sterile field drape, abdominal preparation solution (Betadine solution), a 20 gauge × 3 inch needle with depth markings, 5 cc syringe, 20 cc syringe, 22 gauge × 1 1/2 inch needle, 25 gauge × 5/8 inch needle, idocane 1% 5 mL ampule, 3 amber specimen tubes with caps, 3 sponge applicators, 15 cc ruler, 3 gauze pads 2 × 2 inches, absorbent towel, bandage, ultrasound machine, ultrasound Doppler device, and an electronic fetal monitor for gestations greater than 20 weeks.

Procedure and Rationale

1. Check and document blood type and Rh status. Women who are Rh negative will need RhoGAM, so the order should be placed immediately upon admission. RhoGAM is warranted for all Rh-negative women to prevent isoimmunization.
2. Ensure consent has been signed and all questions have been answered. Ask the patient to verbalize understanding. Consent obtained from the physician is required prior to any procedure.
3. Obtain maternal vital signs; start intravenous line per physician order; obtain FHR and document findings. If greater than 20 weeks, obtain a 20-minute fetal monitoring strip. Document if any uterine activity is present. Baseline vital signs and fetal and uterine activity assessments provide data so changes in maternal or fetal status can be determined during and after the procedure.
4. Position the woman in low Fowler's or dorsal recumbent with a hip tilt position. Optimal positioning aids the physician in performing the procedure and reduces the risk of fetal injury.
5. Assist the physician with performing an ultrasound examination to identify fetal position to guide the

procedure and to reduce the risk of fetal puncture or injury. Ultrasound examination is now standard practice to prevent puncture injuries.

6. Assist the physician with equipment including abdominal prep and specimen collection as needed while providing emotional support and patient education to the woman and her support person during the procedure. Most women experience anxiety during the procedure so reassurance and ongoing education can put the woman at ease or reduce some of her anxiety.
7. Label specimens with identifying information or patient label prior to leaving the room. Proper labeling prevents laboratory errors.
8. Reapply the fetal monitor after the procedure and monitor for fetal heart rate and uterine activity for at least 1 hour post-procedure. If no nonreassuring fetal heart rate patterns or contractions are present, the woman can be prepared for discharge. Few complications occur (less than 0.5%); however, monitoring for complications is warranted.
9. If the specimen is being collected for fetal lung maturity, place on ice immediately, protect from light, and immediately transfer to the lab. If the specimen is for genetic analysis, label and transfer to the lab in the appropriate collection tube. Placing the specimen on ice preserves the integrity of the sample until testing can be performed.
10. Administer RhoGAM to all Rh-negative women and provide documentation (wallet card) for her to carry prior to discharge. If RhoGAM is not given, the woman is at risk for isoimmunization.
11. Assess the puncture site and bandage to ensure no amniotic fluid leaking or bleeding is actively occurring, which increases the risk of infection. Few women experience leaking of amniotic fluid or bleeding from the puncture site.
12. Provide discharge instructions and opportunity for the woman and her support person to ask questions. Women should be taught warning signs that could occur that warrant notifying the physician.

LEOPOLD'S MANEUVERS

Background

Leopold's maneuvers are a systematic approach used by care providers to identify the fetal position in a noninvasive, low technology manner. Leopold's maneuvers are a functional tool to help identify fetal lie and position to determine location of FHR, ensure a vertex presentation prior to the onset of labor in term pregnancies, and to estimate fetal weight.

Equipment

None.

Procedure and Rationale

1. Advise the woman to empty her bladder. A full bladder can interfere with performing the procedure and increase discomfort.
2. Assist the woman into a comfortable position with shoulders slightly elevated and knees bent. Bending the knees reduces discomfort during the procedure.
3. With warmed hands, face the woman standing to one side. The first maneuver is the fundal grip, which is performed by using both hands to palpate the top of the uterus for consistency, size, shape, and mobility of the palpated part. A gradual shifting motion that compresses the part between the examiner's two hands can help identify these factors. In a breech presentation, the part in the fundal area is hard, firm, round, and moves as a single unit, whereas if the buttocks are present, they are softer and feel more symmetrical. If the shoulders are in the fundus, there is a lack of a round object and instead the examiner feels bony

prominences and more soft areas that feel empty or do not contain a fetal part.

4. The umbilical grip is performed by sliding both hands down to the umbilical or areas on each side in an attempt to identify the position of the fetal back, compressing one hand at a time and then alternating to the other side. The fetal back is solid and remains firm under the examiner's hand while limbs lack areas of firmness and appear to have more irregularities and areas that are more compressible. In a longitudinal lie, once the back is identified, slide the examining hand down the back to identify the part that is in the fundus and the part in the pelvis. Comparing these parts to determine which is hard and more firm and round will reveal the position of the fetal head.
5. Next, the examiner determines the part contained within the lower abdomen above the pelvic inlet. Using Pawlick's grip, the examiner spreads the hand with the fingers extended and the thumb in the opposite position and then palpates right above the symphysis pubis to determine what is in the pelvic inlet. Often, the examiner performs this several times to determine the consistency of that part and compare it to the findings from the first maneuver. Alternately, a two-handed approach can be adapted, which is said to reduce discomfort for the woman.
6. Finally, the pelvic grip is performed. In the final step, the examiner faces the woman's feet and attempts to locate the fetal brow by palpating the fetal back and attempting to follow the back to the maternal pelvis until the brow is palpated. When the brow is identified, there is resistance to the descent of the fingers. The four maneuvers together provide a clinical picture that reveals the fetal lie, position, fetal weight, and other clinical factors. Many clinicians repeat these maneuvers in a systematic flow multiple times when performing the assessment.

ASSESSING DEEP TENDON REFLEXES AND CLONUS

Background

Deep tendon reflexes and clonus are parameters that are commonly assessed in pregnancy to determine if central nervous system irritability is present. Central nervous system irritability can occur as a complication from preeclampsia or eclampsia. It should also be routinely assessed in women receiving magnesium sulfate for the treatment of preeclampsia, eclampsia, or preterm labor. Deep tendon reflexes can be assessed using triceps, biceps, brachioradialis, or the patellar. The patellar is the most common site used. Deep tendon reflexes assess the motor response that occurs in response to a sensory stimulation. To elicit a motor response, the muscle's tendon is stimulated by striking it with a reflex hammer or the side of a hand and the response is then recorded using a standardized scale. Clonus is a repetitive vibratory contraction of the muscle that occurs in response to the muscle and tendon stretch and is a characteristic found when central nervous system irritability is present.

Equipment

Reflex hammer.

Procedure and Rationale

1. Have the woman sit in a comfortable position, typically on an exam table in an outpatient setting. If the woman is in bed or in a lying position, dangle the extremity so the procedure can be properly performed. If the woman

is able to sit at the bedside, assist her into the proper seated position. Some women may be unable to sit up and may need to remain in a recumbent position.

2. Identify the proper location where the tendon will be struck depending on which muscle site is being used. Using the reflex hammer or the side of your hand, strike the identified area in a swift, steady manner. If the proper site is not tested, a negative or absent finding will be present.
3. Observe the reflex and rate it according to the scale. Normal findings are 1+, 2+, or 3+. Providing a standardized assessment using a scale ensures that all health care providers have knowledge of the patient's status.
   - Absent: No response.
   - 1+: Trace, or seen only with reinforcement
   - 2+: Normal
   - 3+: Brisk
   - 4+: Nonsustained clonus
   - 5+: Sustained clonus
4. In order to test for clonus, dorsiflex the foot toward the woman's head, letting go quickly and observing for clonus or rhythmic beats that may occur. If no beats occur, clonus is not present. If clonus is present, count the number of beats that occur and document appropriately. Assessing for clonus is warranted to provide comprehensive assessment of central nervous system irritability.
5. Document findings in the patient record. Abnormal findings that include clonus 4+ or 5+ warrant immediate reporting to the clinician since this can be a sign of central nervous system irritability and is a significant risk factor for hypertensive disorders in pregnancy. In addition, the woman with absent reflexes who is receiving magnesium sulfate therapy also warrants immediate clinician assessment and blood testing to rule out magnesium sulfate toxicity. Proper documentation allows all health care providers to monitor changes in the woman's status.

ELECTRONIC FETAL MONITORING

Background

Electronic fetal monitoring (EFM) is used frequently to provide ongoing monitoring of the fetal status. Although the procedure is widely used, it has not been shown to be superior to intermittent fetal monitoring for low-risk women and has not reduced adverse fetal outcomes or reduced operative delivery rates.

Equipment

EFM unit, two monitoring belts, ultrasound conduction gel.

Procedure and Rationale

1. Assist the woman into a comfortable position. The woman is usually recumbent and should have the left hip slightly tilted to increase uteroplacental perfusion.
2. Perform Leopold's maneuvers to determine fetal position and determine the likely site for auscultation of the FHR. The FHR is heard most clearly over the fetal back. Leopold's maneuvers provide more accurate placement and provide other needed assessment data.
3. Label the EFM strip (if a paper tracing is being used) with the pertinent patient data or patient label. It is imperative that all fetal monitoring strips are labeled.
4. Apply the monitoring belts behind the woman's back and around her abdomen so they are in place once the monitor is placed properly.
5. Turn the monitor on and place the Doppler disk over the location of the fetal heart. Once the heart beat is obtained, secure the Doppler disk in place with the monitoring belt.

6. Place the tocodynameter (toco) on the top of the fundus when the uterus is in a relaxed state. If the woman is experiencing a contraction, wait until the uterus is relaxed before applying the belt and the toco. Applying it during a contraction will yield false readings.
7. Once the monitors are in place, observe the monitoring strip to ensure that the FHR is being recorded continuously. If the woman is experiencing contractions, ensure that the contractions are being recorded as they occur. If contractions are not being recorded, the toco needs to be adjusted. The toco monitor may need several adjustments to ensure it is properly recording contractions.
8. Ask the woman to advise when a contraction occurs and palpate the uterus to ensure the toco is detecting contractions. The external toco can provide information about contraction frequency and duration, but cannot provide data on the intensity.
9. The nurse determines the intensity by palpating the contraction with the pads of the fingers during a contraction. Palpate the entire contraction paying close attention to the firmness of the uterus at the acme (most intense point) of the contraction. A mild contraction has the same consistency as the end of your nose and the nurse can easily indent the abdomen. A moderate contraction has the same consistency as the chin. A strong contraction is similar to the forehead where there is little ability to compress the abdomen and indent the area. The intensity should be documented as mild, moderate, or strong in the patient record.
10. Once the monitoring has been initiated, the FHR range, variability, presence of contractions, decelerations, and accelerations should be documented. The tracing category (I, II, or III) should also be documented. If continuous fetal monitoring is used, it is important to properly document ongoing parameters of the FHR and uterine contraction patterns.

INTERMITTENT FETAL MONITORING

Background

Intermittent fetal monitoring in the antepartum period is sometimes used to establish FHR patterns and responses to various pregnancy conditions. Intermittent monitoring during labor is appropriate for low-risk women during labor and birth. It is less frequently used during antepartum assessment, although if ordered or indicated, it can be used to gather assessment data.

Equipment

Ultrasound Doppler, ultrasound conduction gel.

Procedure and Rationale

1. Assist the woman into a comfortable position. The woman is usually recumbent and should have the left hip slightly tilted to increase uteroplacental perfusion.
2. Perform Leopold's maneuvers to determine fetal position and determine the likely site for auscultation of the FHR. The FHR is heard most clearly over the fetal back. Leopold's maneuvers provide more accurate location and other needed assessment data.
3. Apply the ultrasound conduction gel onto the end of the Doppler. Conduction gel increases the detection of sound waves so the fetal heart beat can be heard.
4. Slowly roll the Doppler over the identified location until the FHR is detected. The normal FHR range is 110 to 160 bpm. Listen to the FHR for 30 to 60 seconds to determine the rate, rhythm, and if any abnormalities are present. Abnormalities in the rhythm could indicate a cardiac abnormality and warrant additional assessment.

Tachycardia or bradycardia are abnormal and also warrant additional assessment. Inability to locate the FHR warrants a STAT call to the attending clinician.

5. For women having contractions or who are in labor, it is necessary to listen throughout the contraction and after the completion of the contraction to detect if any late decelerations are occurring. The detection of late decelerations warrants switching to continuous EFM and notification of the clinician of abnormalities.
6. If any type of abnormalities are identified, continuous EFM should be initiated and the findings should be immediately reported to the clinician.
7. Document the findings in the patient record.

NONSTRESS TESTING

Background

A nonstress test (NST) is a noninvasive means of establishing fetal well-being. NSTs are routinely performed on women with risk factors for adverse fetal outcomes including hypertensive disorders, diabetes, placental alterations, postdate gestations, multiple births, preexisting medical conditions, past history of stillbirth, and certain fetal disorders.

Equipment

EFM, two monitoring belts, ultrasound conduction gel, artificial larynx.

Procedure and Rationale

1. Advise the woman to empty her bladder prior to beginning the test so the test will not have to be discontinued to empty her bladder.

2. Assess if the woman has recently smoked since this can result in an unfavorable test result. Women should refrain from smoking prior to the procedure.
3. Document gestational age. Fetuses between 24 and 28 gestational weeks have a 50% nonreactive test rate due to prematurity of the nervous system. Fetuses between 28 and 32 weeks have a 15% nonreactive rate even when the fetus has a normal pH level and normal autonomic nervous system functioning. Due to these variations, most clinicians will not begin NST testing prior to 32 gestational weeks.
4. The woman is placed in a semirecumbent position with a lateral tilt of the uterus to increase uterine placental perfusion. Compression of the vena cava can result in a reduction of uterine blood flow.
5. Two fetal monitoring belts are attached around the women's back and secured over the uterus to monitor the FHR and uterine contractility.
6. Perform Leopold's maneuvers to identify fetal position so the FHR monitor can be secured over the fetal back or thorax for optimal conduction.
7. Place the belt around the monitor to secure it in place so that a continuous FHR tracing can be obtained.
8. Palpate the uterus and place the toco device over the fundus of the uterus. Have the woman cough to determine if the device is detecting uterine contractility since this creates a muscle contraction.
9. Monitor the woman for at least 20 minutes. NSTs are categorized as reactive or nonreactive. A *reactive NST* has two separate time periods that have an increase in the FHR of at least 15 beats over the baseline rate and last for at least 15 seconds in a 20-minute time period. Failure to obtain two increases of this duration after a 40-minute period results in a *nonreactive NST* result.
10. Failure to obtain a reactive NST can be related to the fetal sleep cycle so the test can be extended an additional 40 minutes. Even when the exam is extended, the two accelerations must occur within a 20-minute period to meet the criteria for reactivity.

11. Acoustic stimulation can also be performed by providing external sounds using an artificial larynx, which can result in stimulating the sleeping or inactive fetus. The stimulation can be provided for 1 to 2 seconds to the maternal abdomen and increased to up to 3 seconds on three separate occasions to stimulate the fetus.
12. A continued nonreactive NST warrants additional testing, which should be ordered by the clinician. This may include repeat NST or a biophysical test. Ongoing assessment is needed to ensure reassuring fetal status.
13. Document the findings in the patient record.

CONTRACTION STRESS TESTING

Background

A contraction stress test (CST) monitors the fetal response of the FHR to uterine contractions. Since fetal oxygenation is reduced during a uterine contraction, the test detects a FHR that indicates the fetus is compromised during uterine contractions.

Equipment

EFM, ultrasound conduction gel, monitoring belts, electric or manual breast pump, supplies for intravenous (IV) access and IV line, 1 L of lactated Ringer's or other IV solution, Pitocin, 500 cc bag of IV solution.

Procedure and Rationale

1. Advise the woman to empty her bladder prior to beginning the test to ensure the test will not have to be discontinued to empty her bladder.

2. Place two monitoring belts around the woman so the external monitor can be applied with the woman in a left tilt lateral recumbent position to avoid pressure on the vena cava, which can reduce uterine blood flow.
3. Perform Leopold's maneuvers to identify the fetal position so the FHR monitor can be secured over the fetal back or thorax for optimal conduction.
4. Place the belt around the monitor to secure it in place so a continuous FHR tracing can be obtained.
5. Palpate the uterus and place the toco device over the fundus of the uterus. Have the woman cough to determine if the device is detecting uterine contractility since this creates a muscle contraction.
6. Monitor the uterine contraction pattern. In order to perform the test, there must be three contractions of 40-second duration or more in a 10-minute period. If contractions are less frequent, stimulation can be provided via nipple stimulation or intravenous diluted Pitocin.
7. Nipple stimulation can be performed by either having the woman roll her nipple for 2 minutes or until a contraction occurs and can then be repeated until the desired pattern is obtained. Alternatively, a breast pump can be applied in which the pump is operated for a 2-minute period or until a contraction occurs and is then removed. The pump is used in the same manner until the desired pattern is achieved. Breast stimulation reduces testing time over IV Pitocin and is a less invasive technique.
8. If nipple stimulation is unsuccessful or if IV Pitocin is preferred, an IV infusion of dilute oxytocin at a rate of 0.5 mU/min and doubled every 20 minutes until an adequate contraction pattern is achieved.
9. After 10 minutes with three contractions of at least 40-second duration, the FHR is examined. If no decelerations are present, the test is negative, meaning no late or significant variable decelerations are present. If the test is positive, late decelerations following 50% or more of the contractions are occurring (even if the contraction frequency is fewer than three in 10 minutes). In an

equivocal-suspicious finding, intermittent late decelerations or significant variable decelerations are occurring. In a test that is equivocal-hyperstimulatory, the FHR shows decelerations that occur in the presence of contractions that are more frequent than every 2 minutes or lasting longer than 90 seconds. An unsatisfactory result indicates that fewer than three contractions in 10 minutes are occurring or the tracing is uninterpretable.

10. The desired result on a CST is negative. Other findings warrant additional interventions, which typically include performing a biophysical profile to provide a more comprehensive assessment of the fetal status.
11. All findings should be documented in the patient record. Findings other than negative warrant documentation of follow-up interventions or testing that is being performed.

Postpartum Clinical Skills

Postpartum clinical skills are essential for the postpartum nurse to adequately care for the new mother. Proper technique aids in the identification of early problems, prevents infection, and teaches self-care measures that the mother will need to learn for proper care at home after discharge.

BREASTFEEDING ASSISTANCE

Background

New mothers benefit from early breastfeeding instruction to ensure proper positioning, adequate latch-on, and proper holding techniques, which can increase breastfeeding success.

Equipment

Nursing bra, nursing pads.

Procedure and Rationale

1. Assist the mother with obtaining a proper position for the infant. Football hold, cradle hold, and side-lying positioning can be used. The infant's ear, hip, and side of the knee should be in symmetrical alignment to prevent the mouth from pulling off the nipple and breaking the latch due to poor positioning. Pillows, specially designed nursing pillows, or blankets or towels can be rolled to support the infant into a properly aligned position.
2. Demonstrate techniques that enable the newborn to open the mouth wide enough to facilitate proper latch on. The nipple can be used to push down the lower lip. Once the infant opens the mouth, a scooping motion should be used to get the bottom lip to make contact with the underside of the nipple while the top lip is latched above the nipple.
3. Encourage the mother to get as much of the areola into the infant mouth as possible.
4. If slippage occurs, the mother should place her pointer finger in a hook-like position pulling outward from the nipple to break the latch and then replace the infant on the nipple using the proper latch-on technique.
5. If the infant falls asleep during nursing, the infant should be stimulated to wake up and continue nursing. The mother can gently move her hand to change the position slightly as a means of stimulating and waking the baby. When the mother is unable to reawaken the infant, the mother should break the latch-on and burp the infant over her shoulder, reawaken the infant, and place the infant on the other breast to continue feeding.
6. The mother should be advised to track the amount of time on each breast. Counting diapers to ensure adequate hydration can be a means to reassure the mother that the baby is feeding enough. Infants that have 6 to 10 wet diapers per day are obtaining adequate fluid amounts. Breastfed infants usually have more frequent bowel movements with constipation usually not occurring. Stools from breast milk are a yellow, mustard-seed-like

loose consistency without a foul odor. Breastfed infants should be fed every 2 to 3 hours with a long stretch at night. Unless advised by a pediatric provider, infants should not be awakened at night for feedings.

BREAST CARE INSTRUCTION FOR BREASTFEEDING MOTHERS

Background

Breastfeeding mothers should be provided with teaching on the proper care of breasts during lactation.

Procedure and Rationale

1. Wear a nursing bra for support and to relieve discomfort. Some women may sleep in a bra at night as well.
2. After nursing, rub the milk or colostrum into the nipple and allow the nipple to air dry.
3. If using nursing pads, remove pads immediately if they become saturated or damp since this can provide an environment for yeast to grow.
4. Wash breasts with water avoiding using soap directly on nipples since soap can dry the nipples making them more prone to cracking.
5. If shooting pain; areas of redness, tenderness, or warmth; or high fever or flu-like symptoms occur, advise the woman to consult the clinician immediately since these symptoms often warrant pharmacological intervention.
6. Cracking and bleeding nipples are often caused by incomplete attachment of the baby's mouth onto the nipple. Lanolin cream can be used sparingly if cracking or bleeding occurs.
7. If breastfeeding problems or breast symptoms persist, encourage the mother to consult a lactation consultant.

8. A hard red area can indicate a plugged duct. Massage the area completely and place warm compresses and continue feeding the baby to resolve the clogged duct. Unresolved clogged ducts can lead to a breast abscess, which requires surgical intervention.
9. When possible, the nurse should observe a feeding so guidance on proper technique and positioning can be provided.
10. Document teaching and patient understanding in the patient's chart.

BREAST CARE OF NON-NURSING MOTHERS

Background

Non-nursing mothers will experience breast engorgement as the milk comes in. Interventions to cope with discomfort and reduce milk production can increase comfort.

Equipment

Tight-fitting bra, breast binder (if desired).

Procedure and Rationale

1. Inspect breasts for engorgement, redness, and tenderness.
2. Advise the mother to put on a tight-fitting bra or binder (if desired).
3. Mother should be advised not to express milk to check if milk is still present since this will stimulate milk production.
4. Do not face the hot shower and expose breasts to warm and hot water in the shower or bath since this will stimulate milk production.
5. Ice packs can be applied to reduce milk production and decrease discomfort.

6. Parboiled cabbage leaves that have been refrigerated can be placed inside the bra to reduce milk production.
7. Document teaching and breast exam in the patient chart.

FUNDAL MASSAGE FOR UTERINE ATONY

Background

Uterine atony occurs when the uterus fails to remain well contracted in the postpartum period. Uterine atony can result in postpartum hemorrhage. Prompt response to uterine atony can reduce blood loss and adverse maternal outcomes.

Procedure and Rationale

1. Assess uterine position, tone, and amount of bleeding.
2. Massage the uterus using a kneading motion on the top of the fundus while supporting the bottom at the underside of the uterus. Continue uterine massage while assessing if the uterus is firming up or continuing to remain boggy. If boggy, call for assistance, and continue uterine massage.
3. Assess if the bladder is full. If a full bladder is identified, empty the bladder immediately.
4. Observe the amount of bleeding that has occurred and if clots are present. A rough estimate to determine the amount of lochia can be performed by weighing the saturated pads and underpad. For the most accurate calculation, weigh clean pads and underpad to determine estimated weight and subtract to find the difference. Approximately 1 g = 1 cc.
5. Obtain a set of vital signs to determine if changes have occurred as a result of blood loss.
6. Notify the clinician of patient status. If bogginess occurs more than once, an order for intravenous access may be obtained. Pharmacological interventions may be warranted as well.

7. If heavy bleeding occurs in the presence of a firm uterus, a sulcus tear or cervical laceration needs to be ruled out, which requires bedside clinician consultation.
8. Ongoing assessments at least every 15 minutes for the next 1 hour are warranted.
9. Document all findings in the patient chart including responses and any orders provided by the clinician.

PERINEAL HYGIENE MEASURES

Background

Perineal hygiene measures help keep the perineum and vaginal area clean and reduce the risk of infection while providing comfort measures.

Equipment

Peribottle, soap or betadine or other cleansing agent, topical analgesic agents, witch hazel pads, sanitary pads.

Procedure and Rationale

1. Have the woman empty her bladder or have a bowel movement as usual.
2. Fill the disposable squirt bottle, known as a peribottle, with warm water and appropriate cleaning solution. Squirt the warm solution over the vagina, perineum, and rectal area.
3. Encourage the woman who has had a vaginal birth to pat gently and not use a wiping motion on the perineum area to dry the area.
4. If topical creams, foams, or sprays have been ordered, apply the medication at this time.

5. Using a clean sanitary pad, have the woman place the pad in her undergarments. Pads should be changed each time she uses the bathroom to prevent contamination and reduce the risk of infection. Saturated pads should be placed in a red bag since they contain body fluids.
6. Witch hazel pads can be placed on the pad and left in place to provide comfort and reduce pain.
7. Advise the woman to report an increase in bleeding, presence of clots, or foul smelling odor immediately.
8. Document that the teaching was performed and that the woman verbalized understanding.

POSTPARTUM PHYSICAL EXAM (BUBBLE-HE)

Background

The postpartum physical exam is performed using a systematic head-to-toe approach to examine all vital reproductive-related structures. Ongoing physical assessment is needed from the time of birth until the woman is discharged from the birthing facility. Using the mnemonic BUBBLE-HE, the nurse can remember key components of the exam and ensure that the exam is always performed in the same manner.

Equipment

Gloves.

Procedure and Rationale

1. Have the woman empty her bladder prior to the assessment. The nurse dons clean gloves.
2. Provide a generalized overview that includes a general assessment, mental status, vital signs, and a pain assessment.

3. *Breasts*: Palpate the breasts to determine if they are soft, filling, full, or engorged. Most women will have soft or filling breasts since the milk does not come in until 2 to 5 days after birth. Engorged breasts feel like the breast is overly full with gravel-like areas that are tender to touch. Document if the nipples are protruding, flat, or inverted. Flat or inverted nipples often warrant a lactation consult in breastfeeding mothers since specialized interventions may be warranted.
4. *Uterus*: The uterus should be assessed to determine position, consistency, and size. The uterus is palpated using the side of the hand, curving it inward toward the woman's spine in a gentle continuous manner starting at the umbilicus. Women often note sensitivity during the palpation, especially if they have undergone a cesarean birth. The uterus is midway between the umbilicus and the symphysis pubis immediately after birth and should be firm and midline. Within 12 hours postpartum, the uterus is at the umbilicus or 1 fingerbreadth above the umbilicus, firm, and midline. After the first 24 hours, the uterus should descend 1 fingerbreadth below the umbilicus until approximately day 10 when it should no longer be palpated from the abdomen. A uterus that is boggy (or not firm and ball-like) occurs when the uterus is relaxed and results in heavy bleeding and postpartum hemorrhage. If the uterus is shifted to the left side, a full bladder is usually suspected. Since a full bladder often results in heavier bleeding, the woman should be advised to empty her bladder frequently.
5. *Bowel*: The status of the bowel is assessed by asking the woman if she has had a bowel movement or passed flatus, by palpating the abdomen to determine if it is soft or distended, and by auscultating for bowel sounds. The abdomen should be soft and nondistended and the woman should be passing flatus during the early postpartum period. A distended abdomen is likely due to the inability to pass flatus warranting a suppository or other pharmacological intervention. An abdominal assessment should also include visualization of the cesarean

dressing or incision if the dressing has been removed. The dressing may have some drainage noted but ongoing drainage and an increased area of dressing saturation is considered abnormal. The incision should be clean, dry, intact without bleeding, drainage, pus, redness, odor, or gaps at the incision line.

6. *Bladder*: The bladder should be palpated above the symphysis pubis. If palpable, the woman should be advised to empty her bladder at that time and every 2 to 3 hours. Increased urination is related to postpartum elimination of excess body fluids and the intravenous fluids that were provided during labor and birth.
7. *Lochia*: Women will have a moderate flow of earthy-smelling lochia after birth. Women who have had a cesarean birth have less lochia than women who give birth vaginally. A moderate flow occurs, which includes flow rates of less than 2 pads per hour. A flow that requires more than 2 pads per hour or lochia that is associated with clots is considered abnormal and warrants further assessment.
8. *Episiotomy*: The episiotomy site should be visualized by having the woman turn to her side and lifting her leg in an upward motion with her knee slightly bent. The site should be intact and sutures should be well approximated and should not be strained by edema. Minor edema or mild bruising may occur. Hematomas or taunt sutures that have occurred due to excessive edema are considered abnormal.
9. *Hemorrhoids*: Hemorrhoids may occur as a result of labor or may have been present during pregnancy. Hemorrhoids should be assessed and documented. Topical medications should be provided. Some hemorrhoids that are small in size may be able to be gently replaced back into the rectum.
10. *Extremities/Emotions*: The extremities should be assessed for edema, redness, pain, or localized areas of warmth, which could indicate a deep vein thrombosis. Normal muscle fatigue and strain are common from exaggerated positioning that may occur during the birth. Emotional

variations occur in the postpartum period. Nurses should assess for the presence of depression, alterations in maternal–infant attachment, anxiety symptoms, posttraumatic stress reactions, and mania or psychosis. Although mania and psychosis are extremely rare, abnormal symptoms often occur in the early postpartum period in women with risk factors for postpartum mood and anxiety disorders.

11. Document the findings in the patient chart and notify the clinician of any abnormalities that warrant urgent notification.

SITZ BATH

Background

A sitz bath is a round disposable container that is filled with either warm or cool water with tubing attached to the bottom of the container to distribute clean water and to irrigate the perineal and rectal areas to relieve discomfort and irrigate the perineal area.

Equipment

Sitz bath kit, warmed water.

Procedure and Rationale

1. Ask the woman if she prefers a warm or cool sitz bath. Assist the woman to the bathroom.
2. Fill the sitz bath from the sink or shower with either warm or tepid water. If using a cool bath, water starts out tepid and cooler water is added slowly until the desired temperature is achieved. The tubing is secured in place in the bottom of the container with the tubing threaded

through the back. A clamp on the tubing should be placed in the closed position.

3. The toilet seat is lifted and left in this position. The sitz bath is placed in the toilet with the tubing and overflow positioned to the back of the commode.
4. The woman sits down on the commode and the tubing clamp is opened. The bag needs to be placed at a higher level than the sitz bath, often the sink, a shower hook, or a robe hook on the back of the bathroom door since the water runs by gravity.
5. The bath is completed when the water bag is drained. The tub should be cleaned. The water bag may be stored in the bathtub or shower for future use.
6. The woman is advised to perform the sitz bath three times a day as needed or for a specified period of time. Documentation on patient teaching and verbalization of understanding should be done in the patient chart.

Common Antepartum and Postpartum Nursing Abbreviations

Ab: Abortion
AC: Abdominal circumference (sono)
AFI: Amniotic fluid index
AFP: Alpha fetoprotein
AGA: Appropriate for gestational age
Amnio: Amniocentesis
AP: Antepartum
AROM: Artificial rupture of membranes
BPD: Biparietal diameter
BPP: Biophysical profile
C/S: Cesarean section
CST: Contraction stress test
Ctx: Contractions
CVS: Chorionic villus sampling
Cx: Cervix
EBL: Estimated blood loss
EDC/EDB/EDD: Expected date of confinement, expected date of birth, expected due date
EGA: Estimated gestational age
EFW: Estimated fetal weight
ELF: Elective low forceps
FBS: Fasting blood sugar

FDIU: Fetal demise in utero
FFN: Fetal fibronectin
FH: Fundal height
FHR: Fetal heart rate
FHTs: Fetal heart tones
FOB: Father of baby
G: Gravidity
GBS: Group B *Streptococcus*
GDM: Gestational diabetes
GFM: Gross fetal movement
GTT: Glucose tolerance test
HBsAg: Hepatitis B surface antigen
IDC: Indirect Coombs's test
IUFD: Intrauterine fetal demise
IUGR: Intrauterine growth restriction
IUP: Intrauterine pregnancy
IVDA: Intravenous drug abuse
IVF: In vitro fertilization
L/C/P: Long, closed, posterior (cervix)
LGA: Large for gestational age
LMP: Last menstrual period
LNMP: Last normal menstrual period
LTCS: Low transverse cesarean section
MAB: Missed abortion
MGA: Mean gestational age
MLE: Midline episiotomy
MMR: Measles, mumps, rubella vaccine
MSAFP: Maternal serum alpha fetoprotein
NST: Nonstress test
NSVD: Normal spontaneous vaginal delivery
NTD: Neural tube defect
nTT: Nuchal translucency testing
OCT: Oxytocin challenge test
P: Parity
PMP: Previous menstrual period
PNV: Prenatal vitamins
PP: Postpartum
PPROM: Preterm premature rupture of membranes
PROM: Premature rupture of membranes

PTB/PTD: Preterm birth, preterm delivery
PTL: Preterm labor
ROM: Rupture of membranes
SAB: Spontaneous abortion
SGA: Small for gestational age
SROM: Spontaneous rupture of membranes
STI: Sexually transmitted infection
SVD: Spontaneous vaginal delivery
TAB: Therapeutic abortion
TOL: Trial of labor
TOLAC: Trial of labor after cesarean
U/S: Ultrasound
VAD: Vacuum-assisted delivery
VBAC: Vaginal birth after cesarean
3VC: Three-vessel cord
VIP: Voluntary interruption of pregnancy
VTOP: Voluntary termination of pregnancy
VTX: Vertex

Common Laboratory Findings in Pregnancy

During pregnancy, laboratory values change and vary due to the physiological changes that occur. It is imperative that nurses use the correct pregnancy reference ranges to determine if laboratory findings are within a normal pregnancy range or if variations are present that warrant additional assessment and intervention. Throughout the postpartum period, laboratory findings return to normal.

COMMON LABORATORY VALUES

Blood Component	**Nonpregnant**	**Pregnancy**
Hgb (g/dl)	12–16	11–14
Hct (%)	37–47	33–39
WBC (SI units) × 109/L	4–11	6–16
PLT (SI units)	150–400	150–400
PCV (%)	37–47	33–44
RBC (million/mm^3)	4.2–5.4	3.8–4.4
MCV (fl)	80–100	70–90
MCH (fl)	27–34	22–31

(continued)

COMMON LABORATORY VALUES (*continued*)

Blood Component	**Nonpregnant**	**Pregnancy**
MCHC (fl)	32–35	32–35
Reticulocyte (%)	0.5–1	1–2
Serum ferritin (ng/mL)	25–200	15–150
Serum Iron (mcg/dL)	135	90
Iron binding capacity (mcg/dL)	250–460	300–600
Transferrin saturation (%)	25–35	15–30
Iron (mcg/dL)	135	90
Red blood cell folate (ng/dL)	70–85	70–500

CLOTTING RISK STUDIES

Blood Test	**Nonpregnant**	**Pregnant**
Activated PTT (seconds)	26.7–36.5	29–34.8
Thrombin time (seconds)	16.9–20.9	18.3–26.5
Fibrinogen (mg/dL)	198–314	401–545
Factor VII (%)	79.9–118.7	133.4–229.4
Factor × (%)	82.3–113.1	124.4–164.6
Plasminogen (%)	91.4–119.6	112.7–155.7
tPA (ng/mL)	2.1–9.3	3.5–6.5
Antithrombin III (%)	85.7–112.1	64.2–130.5
Protein C (%)	65.2–89.2	48.7–83.4
Total protein S (%)	61.6–89.6	39.7–60.1

RENAL FUNCTIONING AND URINARY SCREENING STUDIES

Lab Value	**Nonpregnant**	**Pregnant**
Creatinine clearance (mL/min)	85–120	110–150
Plasma creatinine (mg/dL)	0.65 ± 0.14	0.46 ± 0.13
Blood urea nitrogen (mg/dL)	13 ± 3	8.7 ± 1.5
Urinary protein (mg/24 hrs)	< 100–150	< 250–300
Urinary glucose (mg/24 hrs)	20–100	> 100
Plasma urate (mg/dL)	4–6	2.5–4
Urinary amnio acids (g/24 hrs)	—	Up to 2

LIVER FUNCTION TESTING

Lab Value	Nonpregnant	Pregnant
Bilirubin (mg/dL)	0–0.3	0–1.3
Total protein (g/l)	64–86	48–64
Albumin (g/l)	35–46	28–37
AST (iu/l)	7–40	10–30
ALT (iu/l)	0–40	6–32
GGT (iu/l)	11–50	3–41
Alk phosphate (iu/l)	30–130	32–418
Bile acids (μmol/l)	0–14	0–14

COMMON POSTPARTUM LABORATORY VALUES

Blood Component	Postpartum
Hgb (g/dl)	10.4–18.0
Hct (%)	30–44
WBC (SI units) × 109/L	9.7–25.7
PLT (μL)	50,000–100,000

E

Pharmacology in Antepartum and Postpartum Periods

Prior to administering any medications in pregnancy, it is important to identify the medication and the pregnancy category of the drug (Table A.1). Category X medications warrant immediate discontinuation and a referral to a perinatologist to determine the extent of damage that may have occurred to the fetus as a result of administration during pregnancy. Category D medications are rarely prescribed as a first-line therapy choice but may be given in some circumstances when life-threatening disorders are present or when other drugs prove ineffective and the benefits of administration clearly outweigh potential risks.

TABLE A.1 FDA Categories on Drug Safety in Pregnancy

A	Safest: Controlled human studies have shown no adverse fetal effects.
B	Animal studies show no risk to the fetus; however, no controlled human studies have been conducted, or animal studies show a risk to the fetus but well-controlled human studies do not. Considered safe in pregnancy.
C	No adequate animal or human studies have been conducted, or adverse fetal effects have been shown in animals but no human data are available. Used when benefits outweigh unknown potential risk.
D	Evidence of human fetal risk exists, but benefits may outweigh risks in certain situations (e.g., life-threatening disorders, serious disorders for which safer drugs cannot be used or are ineffective). In general, are not used in pregnancy and should be discontinued immediately upon verification of pregnancy.
X	Proven fetal risks outweigh any possible benefit. Never prescribed in pregnancy. Women with exposure need counseling to discuss fetal effects.

Medications with known fetal side effects or associated with birth defects should be avoided during pregnancy (Table A.2).

TABLE A.2 Medications With Known Fetal Side Effects or Birth Defect Associations

Drug Name	Associated Adverse Effects
ACE inhibitors	Intrauterine growth restriction, birth defects, fetal demise
Chloramphenicol	Gray baby syndrome
Danazol	Malformation in reproductive anatomy of female offspring
Diethylstilbestrol (DES)	Vaginal and cervical cancer in female offspring during teen years, abnormal reproductive anatomy in female offspring
Dutasteride	Abnormal reproductive anatomy in male fetuses

(*continued*)

TABLE A.2 Medications With Known Fetal Side Effects or Birth Defect Associations *(continued)*

Drug Name	Associated Adverse Effects
Iodinated glycerol	Cardiac and blood flow abnormalities in the fetus
Isoniazid	Neuropathy and seizures in fetus/newborn, maternal liver impairment
Isotretinoin	Skull abnormality; ear abnormalities; eye abnormalities; facial dysmorphia; cleft palate; CNS abnormalities (including cerebral abnormalities, cerebellar malformation, hydrocephalus, microcephaly, cranial nerve deficit); cardiovascular abnormalities; thymus gland abnormality; parathyroid hormone deficiency
Lithium	Risks of thyroid and cardiac defects (when used in first trimester)
Misoprostol	Abortion, birth defects, premature birth
Simvastatin	Alterations in fetal growth, birth defects
Phenytoin	Cleft lip and cleft palate
Sodium valproate	CNS defects
Quinine	Optic and auditory nerve damage in overdose have occurred in two cases
Testosterone	Possible risk of language delays, autism, impulsivity in male offspring
Tetracyclines	Abnormal deposit in fetal bones causing intrauterine growth restriction; abnormal deposits in teeth causing discoloration of teeth or other teeth abnormalities
Thalidomide	Abnormalities of limbs or absence of limbs
Vitamin A or vitamin A derivatives: Accutane (isotretinoin), acitretin, etretinate	Severe birth defects, spontaneous abortion
Warfarin	Multiple birth defects

Certain categories of medications are used in pregnancy more than others. Knowledge of various medications within each category and contraindicated medications in each category is important for nurses that care for pregnant and postpartum women (Table A.3).

TABLE A.3 Most Common Categories of Medications Used in Pregnancy

Type of Medication	Examples of Medications Used in Pregnancy	Pregnancy Drug Category	Indication	Contraindicated Medications
Pain relievers	Acetaminophen (Tylenol); ibuprofen (Motrin, Advil)	B	Pain relief	Aspirin
Decongestants	Pseudoephedrine (Sudafed)	B	Congestion	n/a
Antidepressants	Prozac, Zoloft; Paxil is a Category D and should be avoided	B	Depression, anxiety, PTSD	Paxil
Antibiotics	Penicillin, amoxicillin, ampicillin, clindamycin, erythromycin	B, C	Infections	Tetracyclines
Asthma medications	Albuterol is first choice in pregnancy, budesonide is recommended for long-term use as needed	C	Prevention of bronchospasm, reduction of acute asthma episodes	Beginning allergen immunotherapy during pregnancy
Antiemetics	Phenergan	C	Nausea and vomiting; hyperemesis gravidarum	n/a
Antihypertensives	Methyldopa, hydralazine, labetalol, nifedipine, magnesium sulfate	B, C	May be used for chronic hypertension or immediate lowering of severe blood pressure levels	n/a
Steroids	Betamethasone, dexamethasone	D (first trimester) then C in second/third trimesters	Fetal lung maturation when risk of preterm birth	Betamethasone and dexamethasone in first trimester
Antiepileptics	Lamotrigine, carbamazepine valproate	D	Epilepsy, seizures	Used with caution and warrants monitoring

TABLE A.4 Pharmacological Interventions for Pain Relief

Drug	Dosage	Indications	Side Effects	Contraindications
Demerol	IM: 50–100 mg every 3–4 hours IV: 25–50 mg every 3–4 hours	Pain	Sedation	Allergy to medication, narcotic dependency
Ibuprofen	200–400 mg every 4–6 hours	Pain, fever, chronic pain	Heartburn, nausea	Bleeding disorders, bronchospasm, acute peptic ulcer
Morphine	IV: 2.5–15 mg every 4 hours IM/SC: 5–20 mg	Pain	Itching, constipation, nausea and vomiting	Allergy to medication, narcotic dependency, epilepsy
Nubain	10–20 mg every 3–6 hours PRN SC/IM/IV	Pain	Sedation, nausea and vomiting, anxiety, clammy skin	Medication allergy
Percocet	1–2 tablets every 4–6 hours	Pain	Constipation, may cause neonatal withdrawal, lightheadedness, shallow breathing, urinary retention	Allergy to medication, narcotic dependence
Tylenol	1–2 tablets every 4–6 hours	Pain, fever	Nausea, rash, headache, low-grade fever, jaundice	Allergy to medication, severe liver disease
Tylenol #3	1–2 tablets every 4–6 hours	Pain	Nausea, vomiting, constipation, lightheadedness, dizziness, and drowsiness	Newborn withdrawal can occur when used in pregnancy, severe liver disease

Many women need some type of pain medication during pregnancy or in the postpartum period (Table A.4). In general, women should be given the lowest dose possible to control pain and discomfort. Pain medications should also be given for short intervals as needed. Prolonged administration of narcotic agents is not recommended. Women who warrant longer durations of pain management should be co-managed with a perinatologist and pain management specialist. In the postpartum period, brief narcotic administration may be used for women who have had cesarean births or birth complications; however, the use of narcotics should be limited to the first 2 weeks following birth in most women.

COMMON PHARMACOLOGICAL AGENTS USED IN PREGNANCY AND POSTPARTUM WOMEN

Betamethasone (Celestone Soluspan)

Indication: Given to women at risk for preterm birth to accelerate fetal lung maturation and prevent respiratory distress syndrome and hyaline membrane disease

Contraindications: Allergy to medication

Dosage: 12 mg IM once daily × 2 days given 24 hours prior to birth if possible

Maternal Side Effects: Increased infection in presence of premature rupture of membranes, hyperglycemia, fluid and sodium retention, pulmonary edema, nausea

Fetal/Newborn Effects: Hypoglycemia, increased risk of sepsis

Nursing Implications: Administer in gluteal muscle, assess blood pressure, edema, and weight. Monitor glucose levels and WBC if woman is at risk for infection

Carboprost Tromethamine (Hemabate)

Indication: Reduces blood loss related to uterine atony by stimulating uterine contractility

Contraindications: Acute cardiac, pulmonary, or renal disease. Cautious use in hypotension, hypertension, asthma, adrenal disease, diabetes, fibroids, epilepsy, and previous uterine surgery

Dosage: 250 mg IM repeated every 1.5 to 3.5 hours for uterine atony. Dose can be increased to 500 mg IM if lower dose is unsuccessful. Total dose should not exceed 12 mg in 24 hours and use should be limited to 48 hours

Maternal Side Effects: Nausea, fever, vomiting, severe cramping, chills, flushing, headache, joint pain, abdominal pain, eye pain

Fetal/Newborn Effects: None noted. Avoid breastfeeding for 24 hours after administration

Nursing Implications: Monitor temperature, blood pressure, pulse, and adverse side effects

Cervidil (Dinoprostone)

Indication: Cervical ripening of unfavorable cervix when delivery is indicated

Contraindications: Previous uterine surgery, sensitivity to prostaglandins, nonreassuring fetal status, bleeding of undetermined origin, suspected cephalopelvic disproportion, oxytocin infusion in use, contradictions for vaginal birth

Dosage: Single vaginal insert contains 10 mg dinoprostone

Maternal Side Effects: Uterine hypersystole, fever, nausea, vomiting, diarrhea, abdominal pain

Fetal/Newborn Side Effects: Nonreassuring fetal status

Nursing Implications: Administer far back in posterior fornix of vagina, maintain bed rest for 2 hours after insertion; vaginal insert should be removed after 12 hours or if hypersystole or nonreassuring fetal status occurs; monitor vital signs and ongoing cervical assessments to document progress

Cytotec (Misoprostol)

Indication: Cervical ripening of unfavorable cervix when delivery is indicated

Contraindications: Nonreassuring fetal status, previous uterine surgery, placenta previa, undiagnosed vaginal bleeding

Dosage: 25 mcg initially, can be repeated every 3 to 6 hours

Maternal Side Effects: Headache, diarrhea, abdominal pain

Fetal/Newborn Side Effects: Nonreassuring fetal status

Nursing Implications: Continuous fetal monitoring is warranted; oxytocin should not be started until at least 4 hours after last dose

Prepidil (Dinoprostone)

Indication: Used for cervical ripening and to promote uterine contractions when delivery is indicated

Contraindications: Nonreassuring fetal status, previous uterine surgery, unexplained vaginal bleeding, oxytocin infusion in place, multiparity more than 6, cephalopelvic disproportion, contraindications to vaginal birth.

Dosage: 0.5 mg dinoprostone in 2.5 mL gel

Maternal Side Effects: Hypersystole, fever, nausea, vomiting, and diarrhea

Fetal/Newborn Side Effects: Nonreassuring fetal status

Nursing Implications: Monitor contractions, vital signs, and cervical changes

Magnesium Sulfate

Indication: Used to treat neurological irritability; relax smooth muscle, which decreases blood pressure and decreases frequency and duration of uterine contractions

Contraindications: Myasthenia gravis is an absolute contraindication. Cautious use in heart block and heart damage, and impaired renal functioning

Dosage: Loading dose is 4 to 6 g over 20 to 30 minutes then 2 to 3 g/hr via infusion pump

Maternal Side Effects: Lethargy, weakness, sweating, hot flushes, nasal congestion, visual changes, vomiting, constipation, slurred speech, palpitations, pulmonary edema. Toxic levels result in diminished reflexes, oliguria, respiratory depression, circulatory collapse, and respiratory arrest

Fetal/Newborn Side Effects: Reduced fetal heart rate (FHR), reduced FHR variability, observe newborn for signs of toxicity and respiratory depression

Nursing Implications: Monitor blood pressure throughout administration, frequent vital signs, hourly urine output monitoring via Foley catheter, assess deep tendon reflexes every hour, continuous fetal monitoring is warranted, magnesium levels every 6 to 8 hours to establish therapeutic range and monitor for toxic levels

Measles, Mumps, Rubella Vaccine (M-M-R II)

Indication: Indicated for women who have screened nonimmune during pregnancy

Contraindications: Positive titer indicating immunity, hypersensitivity to any component of the vaccine, including gelatin; a history of anaphylactic or anaphylactoid reaction to neomycin; blood dyscrasias, leukemia, any type of lymphomas, malignant neoplasms affecting the bone marrow or lymphatic systems; an immunodeficient condition or receiving immunosuppressive therapy; an active febrile illness. Pregnancy within 30 days of vaccine administration is contraindicated because it is a live vaccine

Dosage: 0.5 mL administered subcutaneously, preferably into the outer aspect of the upper arm

Maternal Side Effects: Joint pain, stiffness, rash, bleeding, low platelet count, seizure, swollen glands and injection-related side effects such as redness or pain at injection site

Nursing Implications: Check prenatal record to determine if woman is nonimmune to rubella. All nonimmune women should receive M-M-R II vaccine prior to discharge. Women should be counseled not to become pregnant in the next 30 days following administration. Breastfeeding after administration poses no side effects to newborn and offers passive immunity

Methergine (Methylergonovine Maleate)

Indication: Stimulates smooth muscle of the uterus to sustain a contracted state of the uterus postpartum and decrease heavy bleeding related to uterine atony

Contraindications: Hypertensive disorders; use with caution with hepatic, liver, or cardiac disease, sepsis

Dosage: IM dose 0.2 mg to 0.4 mg every 2 to 4 hours up to 5 doses. Oral dose 0.2 mg to 0.4 mg every 6 to 12 hours for 2 to 7 days

Maternal Side Effects: Hypertension, nausea, vomiting, headaches, uterine cramping, dizziness, tinnitus, palpitations, arrhythmias, sweating, dyspnea, and chest pain

Nursing Implications: Monitor for side effects, vital signs, and bleeding. Administer pain medications to counter pain associated with uterine cramping. Advise women not to smoke during use of medication

Nifedipine (Procardia)

Indication: A smooth muscle relaxer; off-label use to reduce uterine contractions during preterm labor

Contraindications: Allergy to medication, hypotension, hepatic dysfunction, concurrent use of beta-mimetics or $MgSO_4$, transdermal nitrates, or other antihypertensive medication

Dosage: Initial dosage is 20 mg orally, followed by 20 mg orally after 30 minutes. If contractions persist, therapy can be continued with 20 mg orally every 3 to 8 hours for 48 to 72 hours with a maximum dose of 160 mg/day. After 72 hours, if maintenance is still required, long-acting nifedipine 30 to 60 mg daily can be used

Maternal Side Effects: Constipation, diarrhea, headache, nausea, dizziness, lightheadedness, flushing, or feelings of warmth

Fetal/Newborn Side Effects: None reported

Nursing Implications: Continuous fetal heart rate monitoring, contraction pattern, and maternal vital signs including pulse and blood pressure should be regularly monitored. Assess for side effects during administration. Patients on prolonged home therapy should keep a contraction diary and have cervical assessments at regular intervals

Pitocin (Oxytocin) for Postpartum Administration

Indication: Stimulates uterine contractions during the third and fourth stages of labor to aid in the birth of the placenta and to control postpartum bleeding or hemorrhage

Contraindications: Hypersensitivity to the drug

Dosage: Intramuscular dose is 1 mL (10 units) of Pitocin after the delivery of the placenta. Intravenous infusion is 10 to 40 units of oxytocin added to the 1 L bottle of intravenous solution with the drip rate adjusted to a dose that sustains adequate uterine contractility and controls uterine atony

Maternal Side Effects: Pain, discomfort, water intoxication, uterine rupture, maternal death

Nursing Implications: Continue to monitor for uterine atony, presence of clots, and heavy bleeding. Due to excessive cramping, pain medications may be administered. Women with a scar on their uterus should be monitored for symptoms of uterine rupture. Ongoing bleeding when the uterus is firm requires consultation to rule out other sources of bleeding such as sulcus tears or cervical laceration

RhoGAM (Rho(D) Immune Globulin [Human])

Indication: IgG anti-D (anti-Rh) for use in preventing Rh immunization. Given when potential for maternal exposure to fetal cells during pregnancy when the father is Rh positive or unknown. Routine administration following antepartum bleeding (threatened abortion, spontaneous abortion, ectopic pregnancy, molar pregnancy, subchorionic hemorrhage, placenta previa with bleeding episode, or placenta abruption), trauma, amniocentesis, chorionic villus sampling, or other invasive prenatal procedure or blood transfusion with Rh incompatible blood. All Rh-negative women receive RhoGAM at 28 weeks and then again after birth if the fetus is Rh positive

Contraindications: Administration to Rh-positive women or history of severe allergy or anaphylactic shock

Dosage: A single dose (300 mcg) is the typical dosage and is administered within 72 hours of the bleeding event or birth. Bleeds in excess of 15 mL require additional dosages to ensure immunization does not occur. If the newborn is Rh negative, RhoGAM is not administered

Maternal Side Effects: Skin reactions, such as swelling, induration, redness, and mild pain at the injection site. Allergic reactions are very rare. Anaphylactic shock has been reported

Fetal/Neonatal Side Effects: None reported

Nursing Implications: Never administer to newborns. Check patient status to confirm Rh-negative blood type, results of cord blood analysis, and ensure administration within 72 hours prior to discharge. Counsel woman that RhoGAM is always needed following any pregnancy-event, including an early miscarriage

T-daP Vaccine

Indication: All pregnant women, gestational ages 27 to 36, should receive the vaccine regardless of prior immunization history. Women who did not receive the vaccine in pregnancy should be given the vaccine prior to discharge in the postpartum period

Contraindications: Known sensitivity to any component of the vaccine; women with a history of coma or seizures within 7 days of a previous T-daP or DPT

Dosage: 0.5 mL administered IM

Maternal Side Effects: Pain or redness at injection site, mild fever, nausea, vomiting, diarrhea, upset stomach, lethargy, chills, body aches, rash, or swollen glands

Fetal/Neonatal Side Effects: None reported

Nursing Implications: Administer to all pregnant women after 27 weeks, but prior to 37 weeks. Women with no prenatal care or those who did not receive the vaccination during pregnancy should be given the vaccine prior to discharge after birth. Counsel women on the benefits of the vaccination and the need for household contacts and close family members to get immunized to prevent newborn exposure, illness, and prevention of death

Terbutaline (Brethine)

Indication: A tocolytic used to stop premature contractions or tachysystole that occurs in connection with labor, typically related to Pitocin induction or augmentation

Contraindications: Sensitivity to the drug, heart disease, hyperthyroidism, and poorly controlled diabetes

Black Box Warning: A FDA warning in 2011 noted that oral terbulatine should not be used for the treatment of preterm labor contractions and that the use of subcutaneous administration should be limited. Maternal death and serious adverse reactions, including tachycardia, transient hyperglycemia, hypokalemia, arrhythmias, pulmonary edema, and myocardial ischemia have been reported, prompting the new guidelines. Recommendations for short-term use up to 48 to 72 hours to delay birth so corticosteroids can be administered is still supported although once contractions have been halted, long-term use of nifedipine or another tocolytic may be warranted

Dosage: Dosage is 10 to 40 mg with a maximum dosage of 40 mg per 24 hours. Subcutaneous dose 0.25 mg every 20 to 60 minutes until contractions have subsided is the normal regimen

Maternal Side Effects: Pulmonary edema, hypotension, irregular heartbeat, palpitations, nervousness, tremor, headache, nausea, vomiting, drowsiness, muscle cramps, and hyperglycemia. Maternal death has been reported

Fetal/Neonatal Side Effects: Fetal tachycardia, fetal hyperglycemia

Nursing Implications: Continuous electronic fetal heart rate and contraction monitoring. Routinely assess lung sounds and vital signs. Assess for side effects and report immediately if they occur. Monitor length of treatment and notify provider if treatment regimen approaches 72 hours

References

American College of Obstetricians and Gynecologists. (2005, Reaffirmed 2012). *Pregestational diabetes* (ACOG Practice Bulletin No. 60). Washington, DC: Author.

American College of Obstetricians and Gynecologists. (2013). *Guidelines for perinatal care* (7th ed.). Washington, DC: Author.

American College of Obstetricians and Gynecologists and American Academy of Pediatrics (2011). *Joint statement from ACOG/AAP on human immunodeficiency virus screening*. Washington, DC: Author.

Amirkhani, Z., Akhlaghdoust, M., Salehi, G. R., Zarbati, N., Mogharehabed, M., Arefian, S., & Jafarabadi, M. (2013). Maternal and perinatal outcomes in pregnant women with first trimester vaginal bleeding. *Journal of Family and Reproductive Health*, *7*(2), 57–61.

Bagshaw, J. (2008). Women with epilepsy and pregnancy: From preconception to the postnatal period. *British Journal of Neuroscience Nursing*, *4*(11), 532–537.

Battino, D., Tomson, T., Bonizzoni, E., Craig, J., Lindhout, D., Sabers, A., . . . EURAP Study Group. (2013). Seizure control and treatment changes in pregnancy: Observations from the EURAP epilepsy pregnancy registry. *Epilepsia*. doi: 10.1111/epi.12302

Baxter, J. K. (2012). *Oligohydramnios imaging*. Retrieved from http://emedicine.medscape.com/article/405914-overview

Beall, A. H. (2013). *Umbilical cord complications*. Retrieved from http://emedicine.medscape.com/article/262470-overview

Candio, F., & Hofmeyr, G. J. (2007). Treatments for iron-deficiency anemia in pregnancy: RHL commentary. The WHO Reproductive Health Library, Geneva: World Health Organization.

Carson, M. P. (2012). Hypertension in pregnancy. *Medscape*. Retrieved from http://emedicine.medscape.com/article/261435-overview#aw2aab6b3

Caughey, A. B. (2011). *Post-term pregnancy*. Retrieved from http://emedicine.medscape.com/article/261369-overview

Centers for Disease Control and Prevention. (2006). *Expedited partner therapy in the management of sexually transmitted diseases*. Atlanta, GA: U.S. Department of Health and Human Services.

Centers for Disease Control and Prevention [CDC]. (2010). *Cytomegalovirus (CMV) and congenital CMV infection*. Retrieved from http://www.cdc.gov/cmv/clinical/diagnosis-treatment.htm

Centers for Disease Control and Prevention. (2013). *Breastfeeding report card: 2012*. Retrieved from http://www.cdc.gov/breastfeeding/data/reportcard.htm

Centers for Disease Control and Prevention. (2013a). *Disease and conditions*. Retrieved from http://www.cdc.gov/breastfeeding/disease/

Centers for Disease Control and Prevention. (2013b). *Hepatitis B vertical transmission*. Retrieved from http://www.cdc.gov/hepatitis/HBV/PerinatalXmtn.htm

Centers for Disease Control and Prevention [CDC]. (2013c). Parasites: *Toxoplasmosis (toxoplasma infection)*. Retrieved from http://www.cdc.gov/parasites/toxoplasmosis/gen_info/pregnant.html

Davidson, M. R. (2012). *A nurse's guide to women's mental health*. New York, NY: Springer.

Davidson, M. R., Ladewig, P. L., & London, M. L. (2013). *Old's maternal-newborn nursing across the lifespan* (9th ed.). Boston: Pearson.

Fletcher, G. E. (2012). *Multiple births*. Retrieved from http://emedicine.medscape.com/article/977234-overview

Four pelvis types. (2011). *Spinning babies blog*. Retrieved from http://spinningbabies.blogspot.com/2011/02/pelvimetry-can-still-be-worth-something.html

Institute of Medicine. (1992). *Nutrition during pregnancy and lactation*. Washington, DC: Author.

Institute of Medicine. (2009). *Pregnancy weight gain guidelines*. Washington, DC: Author.

Jazayeri, A. (2013). *Premature rupture of membranes*. Retrieved from http://emedicine.medscape.com/article/261137-overview

Kaplan, J. E., Benson, C., Holmes, K. H., Brooks, J. T., Pau, A., Masur, H., Centers for Disease Control and Prevention, National Institutes of Health, & HIV Medicine Association of the Infectious Diseases Society of America. (2009, April 10). Guidelines for prevention and treatment of opportunistic infections in HIV-infected adults and adolescents: Recommendations from CDC, the National Institutes of Health, and the HIV Medicine Association of the Infectious Diseases Society of America. *MMWR Recommendation Report*, *58*(RR-4), 1–207; quiz CE1-4.

Keane, M. G., & Pyeritz, R. E. (2008). Aortic diseases: Medical management of Marfan's syndrome. *Circulation*, *117*, 2802–2813. doi: 10.1161/CIRCULATIONAHA.107.693523

Ladewig, P. L., London, M. L., & Davidson, M. R. (2014). *Contemporary maternal-newborn nursing care* (8th ed.). Boston, MA: Pearson.

Lawrence, R. A., & Lawrence, R. M. (2011). *Breastfeeding: A guide for the medical profession* (7th ed.). St. Louis: C.V. Mosby

Madappa, T. (2013). Pulmonary disease and pregnancy. *Medscape*. Retrieved from http://emedicine.medscape.com/article/303852-overview#aw2aab6b7

Pew Research Center. (2011). *Cohabitation a step toward marriage?* Retrieved from http://www.pewresearch.org/daily-number/cohabitation-a-step-toward-marriage

Ross, M. G. (2011). Preterm labor. *Medscape*. Retrieved from http://emedicine.medscape.com/article/260998-overview

United States Census Bureau. (2013). *Family and living arrangements*. Retrieved from http://www.census.gov/hhes/families/about

Weinstein, K. B. (2012). Listeria *monocytogenes*. Retrieved from http://emedicine.medscape.com/article/220684-overview

Index

CPSIA information can be obtained
at www.ICGtesting.com
Printed in the USA
LVOW10s2149020517
533056LV00006B/301/P